These pages gift us with possibility, with lives rehearsing a living "otherwise," adjacent to, and despite what is, what has been, and what will likely persist to divide us. If our current moment suggests beauty is the state of exception, this book keeps alive the fact that it is the only exceptionalism worth striving for. THE BEAUTIFUL reminds us that Beauty can and does appear as a shimmering of justice, a kindness so common it might just greet us as we make our way down these streets.

– Magdalena Zurawski, author of *The Tiniest Muzzle Sings Songs of Freedom*

"Beauty will be convulsive or will not be at all," said André Breton. In this new collection edited by Dana Teen Lomax, the "beautiful" is exactly that, convulsive and varied. Here one finds hope, faith, and optimism even in the midst of discrimination, instability, anger, and wayward capitalism. The collection is an "act of seeing differently" together. In poems, archival materials, photographs, signs, nature, letters, posters, activisms, poets from around the country choose an instance of what they perceive of as beautiful. Lomax's project is both intimate and expansive—variety and difference become the hallmark and gift of this multiethnic, multicultural, multiracial, imaginative country—how Americans "turn to art to find a way through our suffering" (as Lomax writes in her introduction). What a marvelous, beautiful world it is when variety and difference can be brought together.

– Eléna Rivera, poet and translator

I've been known to ask students, "When you see a falling star, what do you do?" Invariably they all say make a wish. I tell them no, we immediately grab the person near us and point fiercely, "LOOK!" When we witness such beauty, we are compelled to share with another. This is what art is; this is the impulse of the poet.

THE BEAUTIFUL *is a powerful book of witness and aspiration. Each page offers memory, hope, and awe as it affords us witness to the beautiful. This anthology reminds us that we all must be sure to grasp the arm of our neighbor, so they too can know the beautiful is always near.*

– Traci Gourdine, author of *Ringing in the Wild*

THE BEAUTIFUL *is an astonishing, crazy quilt of image, text, and hope that reflects the fragile utopian assemblage of the American political imaginary. In photographs, maps, screenshots, erasures, and poems that range from American Samoa to Wyoming and beyond, this anthology holds up a mirror to our collective and individual historical traumas even as it offers new perspectives on how we might form a more perfect union.*

– Srikanth Reddy, author of *Underworld Lit*

THE BEAUTIFUL

Printed in the United States of America
First Edition

Printing by Edition One
Richmond, California

Book and Cover Design by Roberta Morris
Leave It to 'Berta
leaveittoberta.com

Cover Art: *By Intricate Design*
by Amber Robles-Gordon
amberroblesgordon.com

Visual Art by Marcus Amaker, Karenina Angleró, Thad Austin, Margaret Barrows, Oliver Baez Bendorf, Marianne Boruch, Jericho Brown, Yreina D. Cervántez, Cortney Lamar Charleston, Norma Cole, Ben Easter, Cara Flores, Benjamin Garcia, Cora Green, GreenPimp, Kate Greenstreet, Tim Guthrie, Yuval Helfman, Karen G. (Farnbacher) Hillman, Gemelle John, Larassa Kabel, Stuart Kestenbaum, Denise K. Lajimodiere, Marty Lastovica, Dorianne Laux, Dana Teen Lomax, Stephen Lovekin, Savya Majmudar, Jovan Mays, Aaron Mick, Kristen Renee Miller, Nathaniel Minor, Cassie Mira, Sawako Nakayasu, Julio César Pol, Vogue Robinson, Lee Ann Roripaugh, Tonissa Saul, Sherry Shine, giovanni singleton, Hiroshi Sugimoto, Joseph D. Trimble, II, and X'unei Lance Twitchell. All rights reserved. Each piece used by permission of the artist.

Cataloging in Publication Data
THE BEAUTIFUL: Poets Reimagine a Nation / Dana Teen Lomax, editor.—1st ed.
Poetry Collection/Art   Lomax, Dana Teen 1967-

Library of Congress Control Number: 2021925824

ISBN: 979-8-9850219-6-7

For information about related curriculum, please visit thebeautifulpoets.org

For information about permissions, course adoption, special bulk purchases, or THE BEAUTIFUL exhibition, please contact Gualala Arts at (707) 884-1138 or info@gualalaarts.org

Promoting public interest and participation in the arts since 1961.
Please visit Gualala Arts at GualalaArts.org
46501 Old State Highway
PO Box 244
Gualala, California 95445

THE BEAUTIFUL

POETS REIMAGINE A NATION

EDITED BY DANA TEEN LOMAX

Lomax, Dana Teen. *Matriarchy.* 2021, digital photograph.
© Dana Teen Lomax, private collection.

Dedicated to
Anna Francis Love Lomax
who saw beauty everywhere

CONTENTS

"IT HAS BECOME BEAUTY AGAIN"

— from "The Beauty Way," a Navajo/Diné traditional prayer

INTRODUCTION

Juan Felipe Herrera, Poet Laureate of the United States

ALL IS BEAUTIFUL

All is beautiful. That is all we need to know. If we can see it as we walk—as we gather with the sea, Last Chance rescue dogs, as we set upon the earth in quiet and whirling moments to notice its gifts whether in a Hustle Man ad or the placing of a headstone on the long-lost unmarked grave of Matilda Sissieretta Joyner Jones, "The Greatest Singer of Her Race" at Grace Church Cemetery, Providence, Rhode Island. The Beautiful cannot be buried. The suffering and the Beautiful co-exist.

Beauty returns and expands and can reside on the same space, in the same heart and the same life, as they move, trade places, as the Beautiful ultimately stands in honor of all things and beings. This invisible, yet ever-present luminosity is the guiding light of humanity. Yet we have to notice it, this collection reminds us. We have to see its images pass before us and tear through us. "Move with me," the Beautiful tells us.

The Beautiful whispers in our ear—"We are one."

We are in the Taro and Papaya, the moon glow on the water, we are that ocean sound, and the dog face with tongue flapping behind a Rescue fence. After the floods, after the hurricanes, after the fires, after incredible destruction, the Beautiful finds a way. Even after decades, after escaping Nazi Germany, beauty comes with bravery, with document. It arrives with a letter with more than one destination. Letters have a way of finding the unexpected reader, library, and other waves of breath.

Breath can be photographed. Murals on walls can move. Aerial images can become intimate. A headstone can be placed upon greatness once abandoned. Strangers can become sisters and brothers—in one instant of seeing the page. All is seeing—the Beautiful.

With these pages, we see with others. We see with the eyes of the seer. For a moment, we move differently, we lean and whirl with the relationships of all our relationships at the same time. This book of lives trembling is an offering of what is possible in the present. We remember grandmother, we wait for the ice to harden, then melt. What we always wanted takes place. This is the Beautiful—this is what this volume provides. We are not what we thought—jigsawed, fenced, floating, desperate, housed souls cut off from the limitless.

Yes, we can walk with beauty, among all lives, endpoints and beginnings, above earth-ground and below ripple, moss, and stone—with each other's humanity. Each author here, each photographer here, each moment here can change our lives.

"IF YOU START ACKNOWLEDGING THAT THE LAND YOU ARE STANDING ON AND THE SPACE THAT YOU ARE IN BELONG TO PEOPLE WHO ARE STILL HERE, IT MAKES SO MUCH MORE ROOM FOR UNDERSTANDING ALL OF THE OTHER ISSUES."

— Mary Bordeaux[3]

LAND ACKNOWLEDGMENT

Dana Teen Lomax

The first pages of *THE BEAUTIFUL* feature pieces from the inhabited U.S. territories and commonwealths, places that many people in the continental states know little about, places where Indigenous peoples live and thrive despite efforts to assimilate and destroy them. We begin here. These places invite all of us to deeply consider the land, the places we live, and the people engaged in the processes of decolonization throughout the United States today.

Writing from Northern California, I acknowledge the Southern Pomo, Coastal Miwok, and Kashia lands I occupy while working to understand the benefits I have received and am receiving from settler colonialism. As a poet, editor, and curator, I create in conversation and collaboration with Indigenous writers and activists. Everyone has a role in recognizing the people whose land they are occupying, working together to redistribute resources in our communities, and supporting practices that advocate for land rematriation.[1] As "Honor Native Land" reminds us, "Colonization is an ongoing process, with Native lands still occupied due to deceptive and broken treaties."[2] Curated with this awareness, *THE BEAUTIFUL* begins with work from poets in the U.S. territories and commonwealths and goes on to include contributions from poets in each of the 50 states and the District of Columbia—all weighing a sense of place, history, and the beauty found there.

---

[1] For people in the San Francisco Bay Area, paying the Shuumi Land Tax is one way to support land-back initiatives. See sogoreate-landtrust.com/shuumi-land-tax/. Thanks to Carrie Hunter for this resource. For others outside of the Bay Area, please investigate sovereignty initiatives where you live. To learn more about the land you live on, visit native-land.ca.

[2] "Honor Native Land: A Guide and Call to Acknowledgment." *U.S. Department of Arts and Culture*, Accessed 21 Mar. 2021, usdac.us/native-land.

[3] "#Honor Native Land." *U.S. Department of Arts and Culture*. 3 Oct. 2017, 2:53—3:04. usdac.us/native-land.

EDITOR'S NOTE

Dana Teen Lomax

Top Left: Sherry Shine. *The Journey Continues #2*, 2019, art quilt, paint, appliqué, stitched, some commercial fabric, 36" x 38." © Sherry Shine. This piece is about our journey in life and what we choose to pack and unpack as we move along.

Top Right: *Life Matters*. Courtesy of Pexels.

Bottom: Yreina D. Cervántez. *La Ofrenda*. 1989, SPARC City Wide Mural Program, and Los Angeles Department of Cultural Affairs. © Yreina D. Cervántez.

Crew members who assisted Cervántez: 1989—Claudia Escobedo, Sonia Ramos, Erick "Duke" Montenegro, and Vladimir "Dracer" Morales. Restoration team 2016—Carlos Rogel, Reba Diaz Castañeda, Mike Rochin, Omar Cruz, Luis Tentindo, and Erick "Duke" Montenegro.

Poetry: Gloria E. Alvarez, Sara Martinez/ Rossana Perez, Victor Carrillo.

Photo Credit: Marialice Jacob.

Making a case for beauty in a time of crisis and loss echoes bell hooks's wisdom about love: "It's not about going soft at all; it's about knowing what can save our planet. Which is people connecting, communicating, showing loving-kindness."[4] Beauty inspires this spirit of community. *THE BEAUTIFUL* looks squarely into the past and relies on beauty to rejuvenate, resist, respond. The pieces in this project reveal the poets' urgency to counter injustice, and the work generated from these efforts is beautiful because it foregrounds equity and collaboration. Our painful histories have always walked entangled with tremendous beauty. Each submission offers a connection to other people, to the Earth, or to much-needed social change.

THE BEAUTIFUL began with personal loss. Over the past few years, many of my favorite people died, one after the other. Who better to turn to than poets, those who do not look away from life or death? After inviting poets to send work, I could not wait for each version of beauty to arrive. As an extended family of sorts, the poets offered moments of comfort when so many loved ones were gone.

An overtly political impetus for the project was the awareness that beauty helps us tend to loss on a larger scale, even the scale of the traumas that divide us. Despite millions of people advocating for justice every day, our nation's traumas have yet

---

4 hooks, bell. "Rest in Power, bell hooks—Iconoclastic Writer and Activist Who Reminded Us 'Feminism Is for Everybody.'" Interview by Jennifer D. Williams in Spring 2011. *Ms.*, 15 Dec. 2021. msmagazine.com/2021/12/15/bell-hooks-feminist.

EDITOR'S NOTE *(continued)*

to be fully acknowledged, let alone addressed. We have much work to do. And, in every aspect of our lives, beauty has the potential to unite us. It acts within our psyches in multiple ways: beauty provokes, revitalizes, offers respite. As our world struggles through a pandemic, as many in our country protest against extreme inequity, against racism and the persistence of hate, as fires rage in our western states—limiting access to clean air, safety, and stability still further—many people turn to art to find a way through suffering. A talk by civil rights activist Valarie Kaur titled "Three Lessons of Revolutionary Love in a Time of Rage"[5] lays out this idea: "Our joy is an act of moral resistance . . . Because in joy, we see even darkness with new eyes." Beauty is a form of this elation. In Kaur's work, beauty invites us to look inward, to investigate unexplored dimensions of ourselves, and yes, to experience joy, even in troubled times. Beauty entices us to stop and to feel, to be curious and reimagine, without fervently asserting a self or maintaining a staunch position; multifaceted beauty allows us to sink down and experience who and what we are as human creatures together. Everyone is suddenly silent as the last edge of the sun sets.

"Reinvent the idea of beauty."

— Lawrence Ferlinghetti[6]

In many instances, the art in *THE BEAUTIFUL* is a proactive practice instead of, or as well as, a response to unjust systems. American poet Erica Hunt talks about art-making as "rehearsed resistance," a forward-thinking act that "helps build up a muscle inside us so that when we have a chance to name ourselves or to speak to what we observe, or to call something out, or to call somebody in, all of those things are not just done impromptu, but come from a place of having considered how words can actually convey something when it's embodied."[7] The submissions in this anthology are practiced, embodied responses to a world in crisis. They model how to act and address injustice. Noʻu Revilla's piece invokes the spirit of Liliʻuokalani, her resolve and steadfastness in the face of terror. Jacqueline Allen Trimble's piece pulls us into the beauty that arises when a truth is spoken, the courageous act of truth-telling that opens the possibility for healing. Hunt also discusses the collective effort of all of us trying to "co-create this thing . . . that grows us."[8] Through art, we reimagine what is possible in our communities, what is right, and we learn from this process; *THE BEAUTIFUL* instructs us how to build a world of peace and connection, the world we are actively making at this moment.

---

[5] Kaur, Valarie. "Three Lessons of Revolutionary Love in a Time of Rage." *TEDWomen*, Nov. 2017, 20:15–20:22, valariekaur.com/ted-valarie-kaur/.

[6] Ferlinghetti, Lawrence. *Poetry as Insurgent Art*. New Directions, 2007, p. 7.

[7] Hunt, Erica. "Erica Hunt—George Oppen Memorial Lecture at The Poetry Center on December 12th at 6pm Pacific Time." *YouTube*, uploaded by DocFilm Institute, 12 Dec. 2020, 1:08:26–1:08:53, youtube.com/watch?v=pj6PlPx9Gi8.

[8] Ibid. 1:13:37–1:13:53.

"The more clearly we can focus our attention on the wonders and realities of the universe about us, the less taste we shall have for the destruction of our race."

— Rachel Carson[9]

A friend of mine critiqued the premise of this anthology before it even took shape. And he critiqued it, as only a true friend can, fiercely. Early in the Trump presidency, he claimed that this was no time to focus on beauty, that maybe I had the luxury of safety, but his family did not. Now was a time for protest, for revolt. He was afraid for his daughter. With white supremacist counterprotests in the streets, what could pretty pictures do to keep her out of harm's way?

And I agree. We all need to actively reject racism and inequity wherever we encounter it. Each of us has an obligation to take on what philosopher and activist Cornel West calls "self-interrogation and social transformation."[10] No question. No matter how desperate our circumstances, this anthology asserts that art and beauty offer opportunities to evaluate our actions and reimagine the ways we live in community. The writing often acts as a form of protest in its own right. In the anthology, Karmyn Valentine's poem

"Mikayla" is such a work. Valentine uses poetry to, as Rob Halpern offers in his description, find agency and empowerment—even in the most degrading circumstances. And in Kristen Renee Miller's piece, beauty arises out of communal efforts to provide shelter to women in need even as it holds governmental agencies accountable for their failings. "Poetry," as a mentor of mine insists, "is not merely decoration on culture."[11] The pieces collected here are aesthetically beautiful, certainly. But they also change us, take us out of ourselves, and allow us to focus on or imagine other realities, better ones.

The cultivation of beauty is not a soft skill, particularly in a capitalist, racist system, and it remains a vital practice and a most important one for living together peacefully. When we call on beauty, we begin to heal the wrongdoing at hand. Poet Hanif Abdurraqib's work "How Can Black People Write About Flowers at a Time Like This" turned up in my email feed a few years ago and speaks to respecting beauty. He had heard people at a reading pose this same question, to which he later responds, "What is the black poet to be writing about 'at a time like this' if not to dissect the attractiveness of a flower—that which can arrive beautiful and then slowly die right before our eyes?"[12] This idea of Abdurraqib's

---

9   Carson, Rachel. Speech accepting the John Burroughs Medal. Apr. 1952.

10   West, Cornel. "Cornel West: What It Means to Be Human." *YouTube*, uploaded by Ed Mays, 7 May 2020, 8:44–8:47, youtube.com/watch?v=Aekb3ppKm5w.

11   Deep thanks to poet Myung Mi Kim for all her inspiration and wisdom over the years.

12   Abdurraqib, Hanif. "How Can Black People Write About Flowers at a Time Like This." *poets.org*, Accessed 4 Jan. 2021, poets.org/poem/how-can-black-people-write-about-flowers-time.

EDITOR'S NOTE *(continued)*

addresses our current moment, a time when many of us are watching beauty dissolve right before us in shadows of racism, terror, environmental degradation, and apathy. *THE BEAUTIFUL* responds with insights from poets across the nation.

> *"Our arts and music carry the spirit
> of a people, a place"*
>
> — Joy Harjo[13]

The artists in *THE BEAUTIFUL* were asked to curate beauty, that is, to send a found poem representing the most beautiful event that had happened recently, something from their specific location. "Poem" was defined very loosely, but the work needed to get at something essential, as only poetry can do. Poets could send anything—a piece of legislation, a news clipping, a photograph of graffiti or beloveds or a social event, a copy of an astounding work of art. The poem could be of a deeply personal nature or a collective one; I just asked that the writer not create the piece and that it represent something truly beautiful in the poet's estimation. The poets then passed along the beauty they found, encountered, researched. The rationale in this request was that the writers were witnessing, not creating. Unknowingly, I was riffing on

an idea of philosopher Simone Weil's, the thought that beauty distributes our attention outside of ourselves, requires us "to give up our imaginary position as the center."[14] The poet Hazel White introduced me to this work, and her statement that Weil's understanding is "exactly the radical change we need today"[15] feels completely accurate. Less ego, more communion. This project invited poets to share what they observe and appreciate elsewhere, outside of themselves. Additionally, I asked poets to include a brief description of their choice, to place it in the context of "the beautiful," however they interpreted the concept.

Some common values emerged in the work: The beauty of family, as in Ama Codjoe's piece in which her relatives feel "blessings like a crown of flowers on our heads." The brilliance of nature, as in Jaime Cortez's description of Elkhorn Slough in California: "It is almost gauche how spectacular these landscapes are, they're so OBVIOUS, the way they grab you by the collar . . . shake you hard, and thunder at you." The shared work we have to do, as in Dan Taulapapa McMullin's piece: "Hurricanes, global warming, and delayed shipments / Make sustainability and food security a priority." The vital importance of democracy at work, as in Janet Holmes's piece on the March for Our Lives. The reliance on

---

[13] Harjo, Joy. Facebook post. 29 July 2020.

[14] Weil, Simone. "Love of the Order of the World." *Waiting for God.* Translated by Emma Craufurd, Harper and Row, 1951, p. 111.

[15] Howsare, Erika, "Outlaws in the Garden: A Conversation with Denise Newman and Hazel White." *The Rumpus*, 9 Feb. 2018, therumpus.net/2018/02/the-rumpus-interview-with-denise-newman-and-hazel-white/.

art to heal communities marked by racial violence, as in Marcus Amaker's work: "it's important that we lean on art to open us up to conversation and growth." David Romtvedt's selection, a song in another language and from another country, fittingly ends this anthology: "how happy the morning / of this love." Thankfully, this work answers any questions I might have had about the worth of beauty in a time of such struggle. Each poem in this collection embodies nonnegotiable aspects of beauty. Many of these works look deep into the heart of this country, at its cruel history of colonization and oppression, at the parts of its past that are most ugly. At the same time, THE BEAUTIFUL celebrates a collective desire to belong, live, and work together peacefully. It tells an honest story of a very damaged, very loving place.

> "Beauty is about freedom. Beauty is about liberation."
>
> — Angela Davis[16]

This anthology is about the process and practice of liberation. The pages of THE BEAUTIFUL show silhouettes of what we are learning from our histories and champion ways toward a more equitable society. The anthology confronts our country's horrendous past and underscores people's arduous efforts to overcome it. And therein resides the beauty.

---

16 Davis, Angela. "Angela Davis Speaks on Beauty, Black Women and the GirlTrek Movement." *YouTube*, uploaded by GirlTrek Movement, 29 May 2020, 1:43–1:47, youtube.com/watch?v=fSQ8Oj2_3F0.

Stephen Lovekin. *Words at the Window: Self Isolation and rhe Coronavirus.* 2020, photograph. © Stephen Lovekin.

Claire Ince and Ancil McKain, husband and wife filmmakers from the Ditmas Park neighborhood of Brooklyn, New York, as photographed by Shutterstock staff photographer Stephen Lovekin.

"YES, WE CAN WALK WITH BEAUTY, AMONG ALL LIVES, ENDPOINTS AND BEGINNINGS, ABOVE EARTH-GROUND AND BELOW RIPPLE, MOSS, AND STONE— WITH EACH OTHER'S **HUMANITY.**"

— Juan Felipe Herrera, Poet Laureate of the United States

THE BEAUTIFUL

POETS REIMAGINE A NATION

SĀMOA 'I SASA'E/ AMERICAN SAMOA

Dan Taulapapa McMullin

O Manu'a Tele

Faapea le Motu o Salaia ma Aunu'u

O atumotu nei o Sāmoa 'i Sasa'e

E tua'oi ma le Mālo Tuto'atasi o Sāmoa i Sisifo

Le puna o fitafita mo taua a le Mālō Tele . . .

O Kuki, o se tasi o fitafita tuai o nei taua

Na toe fo'i mai i lona aiga ma lana faato'aga i Tutuila

E faato'a ma totō Isalaelu, latisi ma kapisi Saina mo le polokalama o meataumafa o le aoauli a a'oga

Faapea talo, esi, tipolo ma ulu

E lē faaogaina e le faatoaga ni fetalaisa, pe lagolago fo'i e se fesoasoani mai fafo

O afā, le vevela o le lalolagi, faapea le tolopō so'o o le feoa'iga o vaa mai fafo

E faatauaina ai le lagolagosia ma le puipuiga o meataumafa

Tutuila Island and Aunu'u,

Ta'u, Ofu, and Olosega.

Islands of American Samoa, Sāmoa 'i Sasa'e,

Bordered from independent Samoa to the west,

This source for soldiers to America's wars . . .

Cookie, a veteran of those wars,

Came home to his family and his farm in Tutuila,

Growing eggplant, lettuce, bok choy, for their school's lunch program,

Along with taro, papaya, lemons, and breadfruit.

The farm was never not organic and is not subsidized.

Hurricanes, global warming, and delayed shipments

Make sustainability and food security a priority.

With thanks to Sia Figiel for translation help
Special thanks to Kuki Avegalio and family of Pavaia'i village, American Samoa
Photo by Benjamin Garcia

GUÅHAN/GUAM

Evelyn San Miguel Flores

after dark, with just enough light from the moon and the stars. we'd gone down to the beach simply to wait on the shore while the children splashed in the shallows. standing there in the spectral glow of the full moon, a feeling of deep, certain oneness rolled over me, like rain moving in. the ocean called. i walked into the water, ankle-deep, laid down, fully clothed, in an act of baptism. my daughter and her children, surprised and mystified, joined me. the missing parts of the self, found, slipped into the emptiness. moon glow and starlight from millions of light-years away witnessed the act.

despues di homhom, ya nahong ha inina ginen i pilan yan i puti'on siha. humånao ham påpa' gi i kanton tåsi sin råsón na put bai in nangga i famagu'on mientras ki maná'apalaspas gi i mámatte. annai tumótohge yu guihi gi i gef masåmai na ininan i gualåfon, hinatme yu', taiguihi i ha kékefalulon hit i ichan nu i kumékepoddong, nu i siñenten tåddong. kulan manunu hit—guåhu, hågu, i tasi, i pilan,

i hemhom, todu hit man unu. umågang i tasi. mamokkat yu' halom gi i hanom, achátaddong yan i bayugo-hu, umåsson yu', annai todo i magagu-hu. acton matakpånge. i hagå-hu yan i famagu'on-ña, manmanman yan ti ma komprende håfa i nanan-ñiha bidåda-ña, lao manggof magof, ma danña'yi yu'. i manmalingon-ñaihon gi i espiritu-hu, hu sodda', finalaguai-hon gi i tinaya'. i mina'lak i pilan yan kåndet puti'on ginen miyón yan miyónes na såkkan inina lumi'e' i sinisedi.

— CHamoru translation by Rosa Salas Palomo
and Evelyn San Miguel Flores

Photo by Cara Flores

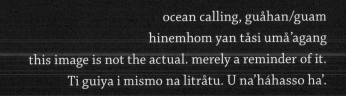

ocean calling, guåhan/guam

hinemhom yan tåsi umå'agang

this image is not the actual. merely a reminder of it.

Ti guiya i mismo na litråtu. U na'háhasso ha'.

NORTHERN MARIANA ISLANDS

Joey "Pepe Batbon" Connolly

Beautiful radar map showing recent storm location:

This is a tropical storm that recently blew away
for which we are thankful in the village of San Jose
they generally form near the Equator to our Southeast
as they head Northwest some become a typhoon beast
now Tropical Depression 22W has moved towards
a Northwest quadrant safely away from our island
hazardous surf, still raining, some banana trees fell down
but in Tinian's village of San Jose everyone is smiling.

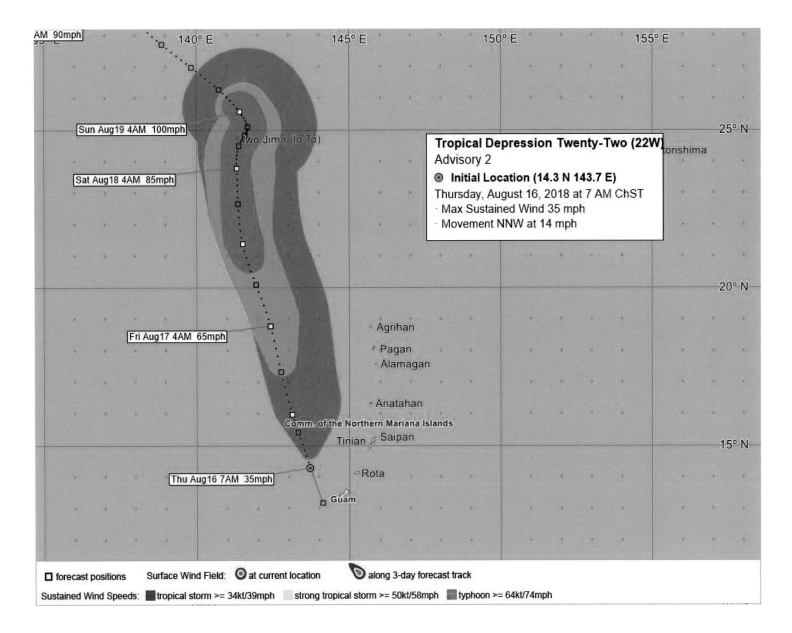

Beautiful! It is moving away from us.

PUERTO RICO

Julio César Pol

La proa de la casa

No había hospitales que la septicemia no hubiera carcomido

No había carreteras que los ríos no se hubieran tragado

No había pan ni lacena

Ni Seven Up ni lata

Pero la falta de luz nos devolvió la vía láctea

Nos dejó volver a hablar

Desconectarnos

Por eso fue que sembramos nuestros viejos en el patio

En las cuatro esquinas

Como fundamento para una nueva casa

Bajo la luz de las estrellas

The Bow of the House

There is no hospital that septicemia has not eaten

There are no roads that the rivers have not swallowed

There is no bread or cellar

Neither Seven Up nor can

But the lack of light gave us back the Milky Way

Let us talk again

Disconnect

That's why we planted our old people in the yard

In the four corners

As a foundation to a new house

Under the light of the stars

— An excerpt of a poem written in honor of the 2,975 people who died because of Hurricane María

Photo by Julio César Pol

U.S. VIRGIN ISLANDS

Tiphanie Yanique

The Virgin Islands is so startlingly beautiful that it would be redundant to include here a picture of one of our beaches, our Carnival parades, our waterfronts of colonial buildings, or well, anything. A hurricane, with winds that knock down palm trees and entire houses, is about the only thing that can compromise the islands' natural beauty. The relief from that beauty, however, also makes it possible to see other types of more nuanced beauty.

This article headline and its accompanying image were texted to me. The novel's cover is of a dark-skinned young girl standing on a boat—she is not a tourist lounging on a yacht. The girl is beautiful, the water and foliage are beautiful, but the girl is fierce and she is heading somewhere fiercely. The book's title, *Hurricane Child*, doesn't seek to present a romantic version of the Caribbean, but rather one that is both dangerous and tender at once. There is also what I know about the author, Kheryn Callendar, who was a student in the Creative Writing Program at the New School when I was

a professor there. She is an urgent, talented VI writer. That alone is something profound, as the Virgin Islands has kept its literary talent somewhat hidden behind its other cultural offerings.

Kheryn is also queer, as is the main character in her book. The recent "We Need Diverse Books" movement makes it clear that there is profound beauty in the reality that one of the few children's books written by a Virgin Islander is a queer book. There is also the beauty of the book's writing, which is only hinted at in the article. And then there is the article itself, which addresses the literal hurricanes that devastated our islands in 2017, the figurative hurricane of the book, and the way that Virgin Islanders on island and in the diaspora rallied around to support our beautiful islands in all the ways we could. This beautiful thing that I found in a text message announces the ugliness of climate change hitting our beautiful shores, but also the sublime beauty of a literary culture that is rising to bear witness to it.

ALABAMA

Jacqueline Allen Trimble

These words appear on a wall in EJI's National Memorial for Peace and Justice. Located in Montgomery, Alabama—once the capital of the Confederacy and a hub for slave auctions—the memorial enacts Keats's pronouncement, "Beauty is truth, truth beauty," by commemorating victims of racialized terror lynched throughout the United States. The words, like the memorial, testify to the power of truth-telling, transforming what was ugly into a beautiful symbol of hope and reclaiming our collective humanity.

Photo by Joseph D. Trimble II

FOR THE HANGED AND BEATEN.
FOR THE SHOT, DROWNED, AND BURNED.
FOR THE TORTURED, TORMENTED, AND TERRORIZED.
FOR THOSE ABANDONED BY THE RULE OF LAW.

WE WILL REMEMBER.

WITH HOPE BECAUSE HOPELESSNESS IS THE ENEMY OF JUSTICE.
WITH COURAGE BECAUSE PEACE REQUIRES BRAVERY.
WITH PERSISTENCE BECAUSE JUSTICE IS A CONSTANT STRUGGLE.
WITH FAITH BECAUSE WE SHALL OVERCOME.

ALASKA

X'unei Lance Twitchell

Hunting at Sunrise

As the seasons turn, we continue to think about aadé s ḵunoogu yé, Haa Tlagu Ḵwáanx'i Yán (the ways that Our Eternal Peoples have done things). This was heading out on the water with the rising sun behind us as we left Anaḵ Yaa Andagan Yé (Place Where the Sun Shines Across; Douglas Boat Harbor) and headed for Xutsnoowú (Fortress of the Brown Bear: Admiralty Island). Pictured is Xéetl'i Éesh Lyle James and Shaksháani Éesh Konrad Frank.

Photo by X'unei Lance Twitchell

ARIZONA

Felicia Zamora

This picture was taken by a local Phoenix artist, Tonissa Saul. What I love about this image is that it mimics the shape of vision—how a human sees out of one's own head through the porthole of the eye. Within this looking out, there comes immense complexities and limitations of our own vision and senses, much like that of a state, which constantly grapples with politics, equity, and resources. To *see* is also a sense of illumination, where dark and light in harmony bring forth truly awe-inspiring visions such as this one. The city-scape of Phoenix set against the backdrop of mountains in the distance, through the rock-eye formation, reminds us of our connection to land, of our naturalness, of our bodies in lands inhabited by Indigenous peoples, our smallness, and the potential to better understand our world, ourselves, and the lives of other people.

All we have to do is look. To *be seen* is to acknowledge one exists and honor this shared existence.

Find more from Saul at deskgram.net/tonissamonster.

ARKANSAS

Dana Teen Lomax

Grandma Lucy said Arkansas is the only state you could build a fence around and still have everything you'd need. I felt that way about her. She made magic out of not much: cardinals on the fence post, sweet tea and fried okra, a ribbon tied at the neck. Her racism jolted me and divided us. The best parts of who I am come from her, and so does the history I work to heal.

I don't know who took this picture, but they must have loved her, too.

CALIFORNIA

Jaime Cortez

The Elkhorn Slough:

In contemporary art, the painted naturalistic landscape is almost genre non grata.

I understand. All around us, we are destroying nature. Painting landscapes seems an absurd, if not perverse gesture at this time.

I understand.

The painted landscape tradition is centuries deep, and try as they might, contemporary artists are hard-pressed to squeeze fresh meaning out of it.

I understand. But I still like landscapes. This one by Thad Austin in particular.

I like that this landscape feels almost abstract. I like the sense of a fast, sure hand working the watery medium to depict a watery place. The slough is one of the brackish Wetlands in and around Watsonville, a Central Coast agricultural town flanked by the extraordinary. In five minutes, one can arrive at continent's end and gaze upon the thundering Pacific. In less than than thirty minutes, one can drive north or east into redwood forests. In an hour, one can drive south to the legendary shores, forests, and cliffs of Big Sur. It is almost gauche how spectacular these landscapes are, they're so OBVIOUS, the way they grab you by the collar like a mafia don, shake you hard, and thunder at you.

"I am nature sublime, mofo. Know me and know awe."

The sloughs are much more mild-mannered. In the twilight, you can hear the Pacific Ocean waters flowing in, out, mixing with fresh water. You can hear the piercing calls of curlews, the chunky splash of pelicans dive bombing the waters. It is quiet and slow there, and increasingly, I ache for that. Most of all, I treasure that the slough looks just as it did when I wandered its shores as a shaggy 70s boy dreaming of going somewhere amazing, without understanding I was already there.

Elkhorn West by Thad H. Austin

ELKHORN WEST.

COLORADO

Jovan Mays

Call it nuisance

menace,
rabies-ridden
infestation
call it, it.

Till the dirt reddens with their mulch,
grounding the ground
to fearmonger the cavalry,
their steed and seed.

Blighted endemic,
eminent imminence,
decaying and renewing.

This is just how denizens dwell,
how burroughs burrow,
how wards warren,

Reminding shine of
how the hood gleams
in the face
of the ravenous masses.

How survival shimmers
at the top of each mound.

The Sentinels.

CONNECTICUT

Rayon Lennon

Why I chose this article:

I moonlight as a psychotherapist/social worker here in New Haven, Connecticut. It's my job to fix what's wrong with the city—which means that I often lose sight of what's good about New Haven.

I first read this eye-opening article in 2012. It was written by an outsider looking in. The article ("36 Hours in New Haven") is close to being a poem—so I went one step further and broke the lines to highlight the music and imagery, which showcase the city. This article turned poem has helped me to see beauty and hope everywhere in the city; and to be endlessly inspired by this new way of seeing.

TWIN LAWNS

A Found Poem [From a *New York Times* article about New Haven by Freda Moon]

It wasn't long
ago New Haven
was the poster
child for the troubled
college town, a place
where graduates of prep
schools rubbed
shoulders with the trauma
of the mid-'80s
and early-'90s crack
epidemic. While
New Haven's hard
luck reputation lingers,
it's no longer fully
deserved. The city's
historic center, which
fans out around twin
lawns planted with
towering elms,
maintains an old
New England character,
with neo-Gothic
towers, well-aged
dive bars and working-
class neighborhoods
of faded but elegant
Victorian houses. While
town and gown have
worked to attract
brand-name businesses

to downtown (among
them a new Apple Store
and Shake Shack), New
Haven remains complex
and layered--a city
of taco trucks
and barbecue shacks
as well as high-end
clothiers and stylish
cocktail lounges.
Drive to the top
of the 426-acre East
Rock Park, where
a 350-foot basalt
cliff offers
a magnificent
vantage for
catching the sunset
over Elm City
and Long Island
Sound, just before
the park
closes. Union
League Café
[features] food
that tastes decadent--foie
gras, caviar
and truffles--without

being overly rich.
Wooster Square
is awash in church
bells and bordered
by cherry trees.
For leaf-peeping,
walk the banks
of the West River.
Sandy Point Bird
Sanctuary (Beach Street,
West Haven), where
birders gawk at red-billed
oystercatchers and green-
winged monk parakeets,
to Bradley Point Beach
(Captain Thomas
Boulevard, West Haven),
near the site of the British
invasion of July 5, 1779.
The turtle-shaped
shell of the 1958 Eero
Saarinen ice skating
rink takes center
stage. Then, window-
shop your way up
boutique- and bookstore-
lined Chapel Street
to Miya's Sushi where
the menu is part manifesto
on sustainability, part
multicultural poetry.

DELAWARE

Gemelle John

Being a Delaware transplant, I was always perplexed by people clarifying being from "North Wilmington" as opposed to simply saying "Wilmington." I came to understand the subtext implied was being from the suburbs, versus the city limits, (once occupied by the National Guard). The "othering" of the phrasing disturbed me, but seeing signs like this in the suburbs brings me an inkling of hope for a broader conversation. The way we talk about ourselves and our history determines the way we remember it. Poetry, as the pinnacle of specific speech, must be a protector of the most marginalized and misremembered histories.

Photo by Gemelle John

FLORIDA

Nicole Brodsky

Florida: The Sunshine (Laws) State*

"Florida Man Calls 911 during Police Chase, Asks for Donald Trump"

"Florida Man Arrested for Kicking Swans at Lake Eola while Practicing Karate"

"Florida Man Uses Hammerhead Shark as a Beer Bong"

"Florida Man Uses Mountain Dew as Fake Urine for Drug Test"

"Drunk Florida Man Tries to Use Taco as I.D."

"Florida Beachgoers Form Human Chain to Save Family"

*The Sunshine Laws allow the public to have access to governmental and judicial happenings in most states, but Florida's "Government-in-the-Sunshine Act" is one of the most progressive, often leading to a glut of disturbing headlines.

Jessica Mae Simmons is with Mary Simmons and 2 others in Panama City Beach, Florida.

July 9, 2017 ·

So what is on my mind tonight?? Boy, do I have a story. And I am writing this in hopes that the thousands of people who was videoing it will send me a copy, so share away please!!!

My husband made dinner and Derek decided that we should have dinner on the beach. So we loaded everyone up (Derek's nieces and his parents) and took our cooked meal to the beach to eat and relax. When we got there, it came down with heavy rains, but everyone who lives by the beach knows that storms on the beach never last. So 10 minutes later, it was over, but we was SOAKED! So we jumped into the ocean (since we was already wet), and that is when police lights on the boardwalk caught my eyes. At first, I thought someone got in trouble for parking, so I didn't think much of it. But when I came out to the sand bar, that is when I notice everyone's direction was facing the water. I automatically thought SHARK. So I slowly start coming out of the water as Derek went over to find out what is going on. That is when I seen the police truck on the beach.. and that is when I knew someone was drowning.... my heart sank. When I ran over there, I found out that they got caught in the Rip Tide that had claimed so many lives before. I knew we had to do something. Derek, Kate (his niece) and some people started gathering people on the beach to form a "HUMAN CHAIN". To see people from different races and genders come into action to help TOTAL strangers is absolutely amazing to see!! People who didn't even know each other went HAND IN HAND IN A LINE, into the water to try and reach them. Pause and just IMAGINE that.

As I start questioning the people on the beach, they tell me that it is not just 1 people, but 9 adults with two small children. I have always been a GREAT swimmer. I was raised in a pool and a lake since I was crawling, so water was no hard task for me. I can hold my breathe underwater and go around a Olympic pool with ease! I knew I could get them to the human chain of people that wanted to help. I went past the 50 plus people in the human chain and went straight to them with Derek right behind me. When I got there, there was 2 small children, a mother, a grandmother, a older son and a Chinese couple telling me they was so tired, that they just couldn't do it anymore. They tell me to save the kids first, so I gave the little boy a boogie board and told the mom to hang on to it. After 15 mins, of me pulling them towards the human chain, The group of people PULLED him to shore like a chain. I took the boogie board and went back in and handed it to the grandmother, who at this point was barely alive. She was so out of it, that we couldn't keep her on the board. She looked right at Derek and told him, "Let me go, just let me die and save your self". My heart sank. I was not going to let this lady die. At this point, the son and Derek are trying to keep her head up. She was so limb, the waves were pushing her around like a rag doll putting her son and Derek underwater to keep her head up. A surfer came out into the rip tide and put the two Chinese people on the surf board which I was so grateful for!! I wish I knew who he was! He got behind the surf board and started pushing it. Derek

grabbed the grandmother and threw her onto the surf board. She just kept telling us to let her be and her son was yelling at her saying, "Stay with me now, your going to be ok!" He kept shaking her to make sure she was still breathing. She was so out of it, her eyes were rolling into the back of her head. After 30 mins of us pulling them, we got the grandmother, the Chinese couple and the Son to the human chain, who pulled them into shore. There was one lady left who had my boggie board. At this time, the EMT finally arrived and ran out into the water to get her. At the end when we got the last person in, our chain grew to 70 strangers holding hand in hand to save these people.

The Chinese people keep bowing their head to me telling me thank you. The son of the grandmother shake my hand and told me thank you for saving us. I had people telling everyone who was involved thank you over and over again! Had we NOT had the surf board, the boggie boards, the HUMAN chain of over 70 inspiring life saving people and just staying calm to get out of the rip tide, we would have never been able to bring them to shore alive.

What I do want to make note of is the 5 police officers sitting on the beach did not even offer to even help or be apart of the human chain. In fact, one of the police officers handed his board off to someone in the crowd for THEM to go out and get them. I understand that officers may not be trained to handle a rip tide and their clothes may weigh them down, but AT LEAST be part of the human chain. In my eyes, it was a disgrace. How can someone watch 9 people struggle in a rip tide and watch them drown??? NOT ME.

What I do want to note about this situation is to TRY and be calm. I knew that is hard, but I was able to count my breaths out and reserve my energy. I was calm because I KNEW they was coming out alive. I knew how to get out of a rip tide and I knew I could swim for long periods of time. But what really got me was how a entire BEACH jumped into action to save these people. People who COULDNT even swim was part of that human chain. They wanted to help that bad. I just wish I could share a picture or video of it. Man it was life changing to witness it.

Panama City Beach, Florida
City · United States

Margaret Duncan and 5 others have been here

Save

GEORGIA

Jericho Brown

Reach Hustle Man at 561-661-9997. If you're anywhere in Georgia, he'll come to tell jokes or cook or lay tile or tell you about the goodness of Jesus: for a fee. I met him in front of the barbeque pit attached to his truck on the street in front of a nightclub. He made me a rib sandwich. He is an example of the everything black folk will do to survive.

Photo by Jericho Brown

7EVEN DAYS 7EVEN JOBS

RESTAURANT OWNER, ACTOR/COMEDIAN, HANDYMAN
APPAREL CREATOR, MUSIC & VIDEO ENGINEERING
Auto Detailing & Pressure Cleaning

HAWAI'I

No'u Revilla

On January 17, 2018 thousands of Kanaka ʻŌiwi and non-ʻŌiwi allies pooled our commemorative power in the ʻOnipaʻa Ma Hope Mākou o Liliʻulani Peace March. From the Royal Mausoleum at Mauna ʻAla to ʻIolani Palace, we activated the intergenerational power of aloha ʻāina. The found poem is a shirt design worn by hundreds of marchers that day. ʻOnipaʻa denotes steadfastness and invokes Liliʻuokalani and her resistance to the illegal overthrow of the Hawaiian Kingdom in 1893.

There is no single artist credit for the image since it is based on an archival photograph of our last reigning monarch and many hands were involved in designing the shirt.

IDAHO

Janet Holmes

I live in one of the reddest states in the nation, where open carry is common, where the governor signed a campus concealed carry law into effect in 2014, and where I have been threatened on campus by a gun-carrying student. This photo shows some of the estimated 5,000 marchers leaving the Capitol and heading into downtown during the March for Our Lives. Their action is beautiful: standing up for life, supporting a youth-led movement.

Photo by Aaron Mick

ILLINOIS

Sarah Rosenthal

I almost chose a photo of my mother participating in a 2011 Sierra Club action. Picture a woman who at age 81 was decades older than the other protesters, her face barely visible above an enormous cardboard "E," part of a "human billboard" that spelled "Mayor Emanuel: Move Chicago Off Coal." But this letter from my father's elder cousin called out to me. Born in 1919, Karen Hillman escaped Nazi Germany as a young woman. Out of nothing but intelligence and will, she forged a vibrant life, first in Switzerland, then London, and finally Chicago. Karen passed away on July 27, 2018. Her intense presence and the challenge of navigating the aging process are both tangible in this typographically arresting document.

June 16, 2017

Dear RosnthAls; *Sarah*

I RECEIVED A VERY ;NICE AND INSTRUCTIVE NOTE FROM DAVID WITH A
BEAUTIFUL PICTURE OF YOUR MOTHER.i DID NOT KNOW HER THEN ONLY
GOT TO KNOW HER AFTER SHE HAD BEEN Married to JOHN.i REALLY LOVE T
HAT PICTURE AMD WILL HONOR IT. i HAVE NOT SENT YOU MY
COMDOLENCES AND AM DOING SO NOW. i WAS SORRY WHEN SHE LEFT
CHICAGO;WE USED TO GET TOGETHER EVER SO OFTEN OR WE REAKKY
GOT ON QUITE WELL, nUT OF COURSE IT MADE SENSE FIR HEr to lIVE AND
Be closer to david who was able to assist her when she needed it.

I understand that Patty visited Saeah not too long ago.; he must already hAve had
Parkinsons which is a horrible illness,

so I am glad she did not have to ssuffer from it for *too* long.

I wonder whether David and Johnny would be able to visit me some time in the future
because I have not seen eithrt of you I AM SORRY TO SAY i WILL NOT BE ABLE
TO COME TO THE MEMORIAL SERVICE.r yOU ARE TOO FAR AWAY FROM
oAK pARK

AMD i AM NOT SUFFICIENTLY MOBILE. i AM SURE IT WILL BR A GREAT
AFFAIR.

PLEASE EXCUSE WHATEVER MIISTAKES I HAVE MADE I AM STILL GETT*ing*

~~MNG~~ ADJUSTED TO THE COMPPUTER..

I WILL BE THINKING OF ALL OF YOU AND i WILL ALWAYS MISS PATTY.

MUCH LOVE *Karen*

KAREN

1

INDIANA

Marianne Boruch

I was reading the local obits to honor small/large doings of fellow humans: the usual *who what where*, number of kids, occupation (teaching, farming, cooling/heating repair) and hobbies (gardening, church choir, roaming the world). Thus a life in quick overview.

This fellow relished travel too but for a most wonderful reason: "and he liked to get lost to know where he was." I imagine him totally disoriented, in suspension = *happiness*! That suddenly opened every door.

Art by Marianne Boruch

Favio enjoyed working in his garden. He also loved to travel and he liked to get lost to know where he was.

IOWA

Akwi Nji

This photograph is one in a series titled *Death in the Family* by a pair of Iowa artists whose process involves the preservation, composition, and decomposition of a found carcass. There is tenderness and manipulation, the repulsive and attractive at work in a way that is beautifully human. I see in it a reminder that we might be as tender to ourselves as we are to the art. The note—a casual one between friends— was included in the same email as the photo and reflects on the making of art.

"It's like swimming out almost too far over and over again. Will the water swallow us up this time? Or this time? How about now? It feels exhausting some days, exhilarating on others, and I almost always end up feeling a little used up."

The series is *Death in the Family*, and this is "The Beautiful Disappointment," 2017, Belle Morte Collective: Larassa Kabel and Ben Easter. Photo by Ben Easter

KANSAS

Megan Kaminski

Citing concerns about water contamination, animal welfare, exploitative wages, and tax easements that would let Tyson off the hook for funding the increased infrastructure necessitated by the plant, the town of Tonganoxie, Kansas, joined together to turn away the industrial-ag giant.

Two weeks of grassroots activism culminated in the toppling of this state-backed corporate deal—and it feels like a moment of hope in a state dominated by a billionaire-driven political machine that works to the detriment of most Kansas residents.

*Not everything is beautiful, though. Some see local resistance as being partially driven by xenophobic and racist fears regarding an influx of non-white immigrant workers at the proposed plant. And Tyson instead built the plant in the comparatively economically depressed Coffeyville, Kansas, where the proposal received a much friendlier reception.

cbsnews.com/news/kansas-town-rejects-tyson-chicken-plant-1600-jobs

Corbin Reischman, 4, holds up an anti-Tyson sign while sitting with his father Joshua during a Sept. 15 rally in opposition to a Tyson Foods plant being built in Tonganoxie. (Chris Neal/*Topeka Capital-Journal*)

AP October 26, 2017, 9:09 AM

This Kansas town told Tyson to get lost

TONGANOXIE, Kan. - When Shannon Reischman takes in the sweeping view from the big hill behind her in-laws' farmhouse outside the northeastern Kansas town of Tonganoxie, she sees a rural oasis that's an easy commute to Kansas City-area jobs.

Tyson Foods (TSN) looked at the bedroom community of about 5,300 people and saw a good place to build a $320 million chicken-processing plant. And when the Springdale, Arkansas-based agribusiness giant announced its plans in early September, residents such as Reischman were quick to mobilize.

But they weren't on social media to court the company. They used their posts to organize protests to drive Tyson away.

Two weeks after the announcement, local officials withdrew their support and Tyson started looking elsewhere . . .

KENTUCKY

Kristen Renee Miller

A few years ago, the city of Louisville tried to shut down a shelter for unhoused women operating in an area of recent development and gentrification. As often happens with social service nonprofits, the city invoked old zoning ordinances in the most rigid possible terms to try and force them out. According to the mayor's office, because the shelter operated from a former hotel only paying guests would be allowed to stay in its rooms.

In response, the shelter offered rooms to the city's unhoused residents at the rate of one penny per night.

When the story was reported on local news, hundreds of Kentuckians brought jars, bags, and buckets of pennies to distribute at the shelter's entrance. One donor, who arrived wearing a Batman costume, brought a check for five-thousand dollars. "I've done the math," he said. It would cover the cost of every resident for five years.

Photo by Kristen Renee Miller

LOUISIANA

Megan Burns

I've lived my whole life in New Orleans. I watched Hurricane Katrina and the federal levee failures destroy the city and then watched the slow rebuilding that followed over the next decade following that event. I don't think I ever even considered the possibility that this city, even with all of those changes to the landscape, would be forward thinking enough to remove these racist monuments. It is truly one of the highest moments in this city's history that it listened to the people of this place and their suffering, and that against much backlash, still made the right decision. Especially in light of the current political administration, it remains a beacon of hope and change lighting progress and growth even as we continue to struggle against a tide of racism and intolerance in this country. New Orleans or Bulbancha as it is properly named by the indigenous people who lived here prior to it being settled by colonizers remains a "place of many tongues" and within the state of Louisiana, hopefully, an inspiration to protect and keep safe all peoples who live within it.

white supremacist attack on the city's integrated police force; next, Confederate Jefferson Davis—a bronze statue of the only president of the Confederacy, mounted on a pedestal in the working-class Mid-City area of town; then, Confederate General P.G.T. Beauregard, mounted high on a horse in a roundabout at the entrance to City Park. Statue supporters say they represent an important part of the state's identity and culture—but in a city where 60 percent of the residents are African-American, many see the monuments as an offensive celebration of the Confederacy and the system of slavery it sought to preserve.

Over the past month, these venues became gathering places for people who support the statue removal, and those who opposed them. The first three came down in the middle of the night; the official reason was for the protection and safety of the workers engaged in this rewriting of the historical record. The contractors who signed up for the removal received multiple death threats, and one had his car firebombed last year.

The showdown bore all the acrimony and divisiveness typical of modern-day American politics, but also carried deep historical echoes: Those opposed to the removal lit candles at the base of the monuments and carried Confederate flags, pistols and automatic rifles. Some came from as far away as Oklahoma to join in the protest. Anti-monument groups flew banners saying "Take 'em down" and even held a barbecue at the Jefferson Davis statue.

– Excerpt from the NPR article "With Lee Statue's Removal, Another Battle of New Orleans Comes to a Close" by Tegan Wendland

The New Orleans City Council had declared the city's four Confederate monuments a public nuisance. On Friday police cars circled the last one standing, the imposing statue of General Robert E. Lee, a 16-foot-tall bronze figure mounted on a 60-foot pedestal in the center of Lee Circle near downtown. Live news trucks were parked on side streets, and cameramen watched from the windows of nearby hotel rooms. The air was muggy and tense.Three monuments already had come down in what represented a sharp cultural changing of the guard: First it was the Liberty Place monument, an obelisk tucked on a back street near the French Quarter that commemorated a Reconstruction Era

MAINE

Stuart Kestenbaum

The Lily Pond is Deer Isle's largest body of fresh water, about three-quarters of a mile long. Winter's freeze is less predictable now than it used to be, so when the weather turns cold enough, we make sure to get out and skate. The first time out on new ice feels like a leap of faith to me, 15 to 20 feet of water below, and the tiny air bubbles trapped in ice looking like they are speeding through the cosmos.

I glide up to exposed granite ledge, where the water from the surrounding spruce fir woods drains through moss and ledge into the pond. It's a view I could never have unless I was standing on water, and here it is. The unexpected view, a slowed down world.

Photo by Stuart Kestenbaum

MARYLAND

Linda Pastan

In *King Lear,* Shakespeare mentions wanton boys killing flies for sport. It seems to me that wanton cruelty to animals, even flies, is not just predictive but part and parcel of cruelty to other humans—in this and any other year. So when I read of a group traveling all the way from Maryland to Texas to rescue dogs abandoned in the path of Hurricane Harvey, it represented to me something redemptive and yes, even beautiful.

Article by Amy Aubert/ABC | Friday, August 25, 2017

Animals from areas in Mississippi that are being evacuated . Courtesy: Last Chance Animal Rescue

WALDORF, Md. (ABC7)—For a group of puppies and dogs at the Last Chance Animal Rescue in Waldorf, Maryland, their trip north is a second chance.

"I feel like, 'Oh my God, we have to do something!' Because it seems so unfair," said Cynthia Sharpley, Director of Last Chance Animal Rescue. Sharpley says it's unfair for the animals impacted by Hurricane Harvey. "The shelters—what do you do? You have to leave," she said of the areas that need to evacuate because of the storm. "You can't leave the animals in the cage. You can't take them with you because there's too many. So, unfortunately, they are doing mass euthanasias."

MASSACHUSETTS

Eileen Myles

Mirror Poem

I was in P-town last summer (2017) on Sept 3rd when John Ashbery died. I read that he had found a reproduction of Parmigianino's "Self-portrait in a Convex Mirror" in a Provincetown bookstore one winter day in the late sixties I think. Parmigianino was gay and the story goes that looking at that painting yielded John's great poem which triggered his legendary poetry-weird massive success. I decided I had to find that bookstore. It wasn't so much wanting to stand where Lightning Hopkins stood on Highway 61 when he sold his soul to the devil (which I *have* done) as wanting to touch John and be another artist looking at an artist looking at an artist standing in a hole in time. Kind of a man. Parmigianino is reaching out in his painting. All of it is an invite. I walked around Provincetown that day all day in the pouring rain thinking about John, looking for the exact bookstore and after many stops and phone calls while getting soaking wet I discovered it was the first one I had walked into—exactly where I began.

Parmigianino, *Self-portrait in a Convex Mirror*, 1524

53

MICHIGAN

Rob Halpern

I've had the privilege to work, think, and write with Karmyn Valentine for several years in a poetry workshop that I facilitate inside Women's Huron Valley Prison. Her poem, "Mikayla," bears witness to an extraordinary set of circumstances and it has everything to do with how poetry can enable forms of agency and self-organization, collective study and mutual aid, while cultivating a deeply rooted—that is, radical—sense of empowerment, even inside the most disempowering of situations. Karmyn now lives and works outside.

MIKAYLA

by Karmyn Valentine

I am not supposed to be
this. Bleached shell or even
bone, yet these are my hands

waving, waving. I know
at the bottom is such
violence. The south

still feels like
home. In photographs
our bodies meet

on granite ledges, but
surface has no color
at depths like

this. All her
knowing of me, all
parts of my

life. If I could
make sense out of
the way water

forms around something
received slow because
I am the same as

her. Even if
our eyes are only
daring the

Mississippi. The threat
of deadly flooding
is real. Like

this pen, is
real. White sheets are
real. Mouthfuls

of black blood, ships
swallowed unto the
seafloor. Beneath

ravens, Thunderclouds,
and white insomnia! You
must feel!

Must see, that we've
drown. So we ask you:
 Are you sailors?

If we had a name, it
would be ocean! and we
would not try to understand.

MINNESOTA

신선영 Sun Yung Shin

Minnesota is a Dakota place. In January of 2018, due to years of Dakota-led community activism, Minneapolis, Hennepin County, the State of Minnesota, and the U.S. government officially changed the name of Minneapolis' largest lake from *Lake Calhoun* to its original Dakota name of *Bde Maka Ska*, meaning Lake White Earth. In 1817, a surveyor named it Lake Calhoun after the United States Secretary of War, John C. Calhoun, a South Carolinian slave owner and pro-slavery white supremacist politician. Starting this year, a whole new generation of Minnesotans will know this body of water as a Dakota place, and that is beautiful.

DATE: January 18, 2018

Re: The Proposed Renaming of Lake Calhoun, Minnesota Public Water No. 27-31 in
Hennepin County, Minnesota to Bde Maka Ska

Based on the information on file at the Minnesota Department of Natural
Resources (DNR), Division of Ecological and Water Resources, concerning a request by
Hennepin County to rename Lake Calhoun, Minnesota Public Water No. 27-31 located in
the City of Minneapolis in Hennepin County, Minnesota to Bde Maka Ska and pursuant
to the authority granted to the DNR Commissioner (Commissioner) by Minn. Stat..
§83A.02 (2016) Commissioner hereby approves the renaming of Lake Calhoun in
Hennepin County as set forth herein.

HISTORICAL BACKGROUND

1.   Lake Calhoun, Minnesota Public Water No. 27-31, is a public water of the
State of Minnesota located in sections 4, 5; 32, 33 of Township 28; 29 North, Range 24
West (in the City of Minneapolis) in Hennepin County, Minnesota.

2.   It is unknown precisely when Minnesota Public Water No. 27-31 was
actually named Lake Calhoun, although references to said name were documented in
Henry Schoolcraft's narrative journal of travels through the northwestern regions of the
United States. Schoolcraft reports: "About six miles west of the new cantonement there
are several beautiful little lakes, situated in the prairies. They consist of the purest water
and are surrounded with a handsome beach of yellow sand and water-worn pebbles . . .
The largest of these lakes is about four miles in circumference, and is called Calhoun lake
(*sic*). It is stored with the most exquisite flavored black bass and several other varieties
of fish, and has become a fashionable resort for the officers of the garrison." Henry
Schoolcraft, *Narrative of Travels: Through the Northwester Regions of the United
States, Extending from Detroit through the Great Chain of American Lakes to the
Sources of the Mississippi River Performed as a Member of the expedition under
Governor Cass, in the Year 1820*, at 312 (1821)

3.   William Keating also references Lake Calhoun in his *Narrative of an
Expedition to the Sources of St. Peter's River, Lake Winnepeek, Lake of the Woods, etc.,
performed in the year 1823, by order of the Hon. J.C. Calhoun, Secretary of War, under
the command of Stephen H. Long, Major U.S.T.E.* (1884), in which it is reported of the
region around Fort Snelling: "a body of water, which is not represented on any map that
we know of, has been discovered in this vicinity within a few years, and has received the
name of Lake Calhoun, in honor of the Secretary of War. Its dimensions are small."
William Keating, *Narrative of an Expedition to the Sources of St. Peter's River, Lake

*Winnepeek, Lake of the Woods, etc., etc. performed in the year 1823, by order of the Hon.
J.C. Calhoun, Secretary of War, under the command of Stephen H. Long, Major U.S.T.E.*
at 301 (1884)

4.   Minnesota Public Water No. 27-31 has been referred to as Lake Calhoun
since the middle of the 19th century. Minneapolis Park Board, *Discussion Item 2828:
Lake Calhoun – Its Name, the History of its Name, and the Process for Changing the
Name of a Lake in Minnesota*, available at
http://minneapolisparksmn.iqm2.com/Citizens/Detail_LegiFile.aspx?ID=2828

5.   On or about, December 15, 2017 the DNR received Resolution No. 17-
0489 requesting that the DNR Commissioner, pursuant to authority granted to the
Commissioner by Minn. Stat. § 83A.02(1) and (3), authorize the renaming of Lake
Calhoun, Minnesota Public Water No. 27-31, located in sections 4,5; 32,33 of Township
28; 29 North, Range 24 West (in the City of Minneapolis) in Hennepin County,
Minnesota to Bde Maka Ska.

HISTORY OF COMMISSIONER'S AUTHORITY

6.   In 1925, the Legislature adopted 1925 Laws Chapter 157 authorizing
county boards, upon petition of 15 or more legal voters, the right to name or change the
name of waterbodies within the State. The authority of a county board to change the
name of waterbodies was permissible only if the name at issue had existed for less than
40 years. *Id.* at 1.

7.   In 1937, the Legislature established the State Geographic Board and
vested it with the power and duties to name and/or change the names of the State's
geographic features, including lakes and other waterbodies. 1937 Laws, ch. 63 §§ 1-5.
This authority was given "[i]n cooperation with the county boards and with their
approval, to change the names of lakes, streams, places and other geographic features,
with the end in view of eliminating, as far as possible, duplication of names within the
state" *Id.* at § 1(c). The Legislature further "superseded, modified or amended" "[a]ll
acts or parts of acts now in effect inconsistent with provisions of this act" granting power
and authority to the State Geographic Board. After the creation of the State Geographic
Board, county boards continued to retain their authority to change the names of
waterbodies through petition, subject to the 40-year limit.

8.   In 1940, the Attorney General issued an opinion letter opining that the
State Geographic Board had the authority to change the name of a lake even though it had
been known by a prior name for at least 40 years. Op. Atty. Gen. 273a, Apr. 26, 1940.
The Attorney General opined that:

No express limitation is placed by law on the powers of the State
Geographic Board in this respect. None can be fairly implied. The
question of whether or not the name of a lake in any given instance should
be changed is one which calls for the exercise of sound judgment and

DATE: January 18, 2018

Re: The Proposed Renaming of Lake Calhoun, Minnesota Public Water No. 27-31 in Hennepin County, Minnesota to Bde Maka Ska

Based on the information on file at the Minnesota Department of Natural Resources (DNR), Division of Ecological and Water Resources, concerning a request by Hennepin County to rename Lake Calhoun, Minnesota Public Water No. 27-31 located in the City of Minneapolis in Hennepin County, Minnesota to Bde Maka Ska and pursuant to the authority granted to the DNR Commissioner (Commissioner) by Minn. Stat.. §83A.02 (2016) Commissioner hereby approves the renaming of Lake Calhoun in Hennepin County as set forth herein.

HISTORICAL BACKGROUND

1. Lake Calhoun, Minnesota Public Water No. 27-31, is a public water of the State of Minnesota located in sections 4, 5; 32, 33 of Township 28; 29 North, Range 24 West (in the City of Minneapolis) in Hennepin County, Minnesota.

2. It is unknown precisely when Minnesota Public Water No. 27-31 was actually named Lake Calhoun, although references to said name were documented in Henry Schoolcraft's narrative journal of travels through the northwestern regions of the United States. Schoolcraft reports: "About six miles west of the new cantonement there are several beautiful little lakes, situated in the prairies. They consist of the purest water and are surrounded with a handsome beach of yellow sand and water-worn pebbles . . . The largest of these lakes is about four miles in circumference, and is called Calhoun lake (sic). It is stored with the most exquisite flavored black bass and several other varieties of fish, and has become a fashionable resort for the officers of the garrison." Henry Schoolcraft, *Narrative of Travels: Through the Northwester Regions of the United States, Extending from Detroit through the Great Chain of American Lakes to the Sources of the Mississippi River Performed as a Member of the expedition under Governor Cass, in the Year 1820,* at 312 (1821)

3. William Keating also references Lake Calhoun in his *Narrative of an Expedition to the Sources of St. Peter's River, Lake Winnepeek, Lake of the Woods, etc., performed in the year 1823, by order of the Hon. J.C. Calhoun, Secretary of War, under the command of Stephen H. Long, Major U.S.T.E.* (1884), in which it is reported of the region around Fort Snelling: "a body of water, which is not represented on any map that we know of, has been discovered in this vicinity within a few years, and has received the name of Lake Calhoun, in honor of the Secretary of War. Its dimensions are small." William Keating, *Narrative of an Expedition to the Sources of St. Peter's River, Lake*

1

---

discretion by the board. It is not likely a court would upset the board's determination in any such case unless it clearly appeared that the board had acted arbitrarily, capriciously and without any regard for public convenience.

The board should, before determining on a change, investigate the situation and consider all reasons for and against such action. If it appears that the public interest would be better subserved by retaining the name the lake has borne for almost half a century the board should act accordingly. If the present name duplicates the name of some other lake, or conflicts with the name given this particular lake by the federal authorities, or if it seems desirable for any other sound reason that the name in use be changed, the board should act accordingly.

Categorically your inquiry is answered in the affirmative, with this qualification: your board should investigate, weigh the reasons for and against the change, and decide what action will best serve the public interest.

9. In 1964, Commissioner of Conservation Wayne H. Olson submitted an inquiry to the Office of Attorney General regarding the 40-year restriction on a county boards' authority to rename waterbodies. The Commissioner referenced the earlier Attorney General Opinion and noted that "[t]he 40-year restriction is not applicable to the State Geographic Board." Deputy Attorney General Frank Murray responded to this inquiry in July 1964 and again stated that the 40-year restriction was limited to county board actions and not to the State Geographic Board. In the case of waterbodies with names used for more than 40 years, the Attorney General's office again opined that the "Geographic Board can change a name in cooperation with County Board" that had existed for more than 40 years.

10. In 1969, the State Geographic Board was abolished and all of its powers and duties were transferred to the DNR Commissioner. 1969 Laws ch. 1129, Art. 3 § 3. The Commissioner retains these powers and duties today under Minn. Stat. §§ 83A.02-.04.

11. In 1990, the Legislature combined the two statutory schemes, and subsumed the county board waterbody-naming process within the general geographic naming statute, found in Minn. Stat. ch. 83A. 1990 Laws ch. 391, art. 8 § 7. In so doing, the Legislature retained the 40-year limit on the name-change-by-petition process, but made it clear that such limit was restricted solely to name changes initiated by petitions to county boards under Minn. Stat. §§ 83A.05-.07 and not to the Commissioner's name changing authority under §§ 83A.02-.04.

12. Minnesota Statute section 83A.02 vests the Commissioner with the authority to determine the correct and most appropriate name of lakes.

3

---

13. Minnesota Statute section 83A.02(1) provides that the commissioner shall: "determine the correct and most appropriate names of the lakes, streams, places and other geographic features in the state. . ."

14. Minnesota Statute section 83A.02(3) provides that the commissioner "in cooperation with the county boards and with their approval, change the name of lakes . . . with the end in view of eliminating as far as possible, duplication of names within the state."

15. Additionally Minn. Stat. §§ 83A.04 – .07 lays out a separate process whereby the county may entertain citizen's petitions to change the names of waterbodies.

HENNEPIN COUNTY'S REQUEST TO CHANGE THE NAME OF LAKE CALHOUN

16. As set forth in Paragraphs 6 through 11, the procedural requirements set out in Minn. Stat. §§ 83A.05—.07 do not apply to the exercise of the Commissioner's authority; however, the DNR has a long standing policy reaching back several decades of encouraging counties requesting that the Commissioner approve a name change pursuant to Minn. Stat. § 83A.02 and Minn. Stat. § 83A.04 to comply with the notice and hearing requirements set forth in Minn. Stat. § 83A.06.

17. Consistent with said policy and the thirty (30) day notice requirement set forth in Minn. Stat. § 83A.06, subd. 1, the Hennepin County Board, on or about September 13, 2017 published notice of its intent to hold a public hearing on the proposed renaming of Lake Calhoun to Bde Maka Ska. Said hearing was set for 6 P.M. on Tuesday October 17, 2017 at the Hennepin County Government Center Board Room.

18. Consistent with the DNR's policy and notice requirements set forth in Minn. Stat. § 83A.06, subd. 4, said notice was published in *Finance & Commerce* the official newspaper for Hennepin County for four weeks commencing on September 13, 2017 and running through October 11, 2017.

19. Consistent with the DNR's policy and notice requirements set forth in Minn. Stat. § 83A.06, subd. 4, Hennepin County served notice of the hearing on the Mayor of the City of Minneapolis on September 15, 2017.

20. Consistent with the DNR's policy and the notice requirements set forth in Minn. Stat. § 83A.06, subd. 4, Hennepin County served notice of the hearing on the Commissioner on September 15, 2017.

21. Consistent with DNR's policy and the hearing requirements set forth in Minn. Stat. § 83A.06, at 6 P.M. on Tuesday October 17, 2017 the Hennepin County Board held a public hearing and took public testimony on the proposal to change the name of Lake Calhoun to Bde Maka Ska. The public hearing was held at the Hennepin County Government Center Board Room.

4

County Board has determined that the renaming of Public Water No. 27-31 to Bde Maka Ska is in the public interest.

30.   Public Water No. 34-62 located in Kandiyohi County is also named Lake Calhoun.

31.   The DNR received a number of public comments arguing that the renaming of Lake Calhoun is precluded by Minn. Stat. § 83A.05, subd. 1, which prohibits a county from renaming a body of water that has had the same name for over 40 years. As set forth in Paragraphs 6 through 11 this conclusion is not supported by the plain language or legal analysis of the legislative history of Chapter 83A.

CONCLUSIONS

1.   As set forth in Paragraphs 16 through 25 Hennepin County has complied with the Chapter 83A notice and hearing requirements as requested by the DNR.

2.   As set forth in Paragraph 26, the DNR's review of the name Bde Maka Ska indicates that the name Bde Maka Ska complies with the protocols of the U.S. Board of Geographic Names.

3.   As set forth in Paragraph 30 the name Lake Calhoun is duplicative.

4.   As set forth in Paragraphs 28 and 29 the vote of the duly elected Hennepin County Board to recommend that Public Water No. 27-31 be renamed Bde Maka Ska after holding and receiving public testimony regarding the proposed name change is compelling evidence that the renaming of Public Water No. 27-31 is in the public interest.

5.   As set forth in Paragraphs 27 through 29 the DNR has weighed the information contained in both the Resolution No. 17-0489 Name Change Package and the written comments received by the DNR as well as the vote of the duly elected Hennepin County Board and finds that, consistent with said vote, the renaming of Public Water No. 27-31 to Bde Maka Ska will serve the public interest.

6.   As set forth in paragraphs 6 through 13 above, the 40-year restriction set forth in Minn. State §83A.04, subd. 1 does not apply to the exercise of the commissioner's authority to rename waterbodies set forth in § 83A.02.

NOW THEREFORE:

Pursuant to the authority vested in me by Minn. Stat. § 83A.02 and in accordance with Hennepin County Resolution No. 17-0489, I hereby approve the renaming of the following geographic feature of the state Public Water No. 27-31, located in Sections 4 and 5 of Township 28 North, Range 24 West; and in Sections 32 and 33 of Township 29 North,

6

Range 24 West, in the City of Minneapolis, from Lake Calhoun, Minnesota Public Water No. 27-31 located in the City of Minneapolis in Hennepin County, Minnesota to Bde Maka Ska:

Dated: _Jan. 18_ , 2018
                                        Tom Landwehr, Commissioner
                                        Department of Natural Resources

STATE OF MINNESOTA)
) ss.
COUNTY OF RAMSEY   )

Signed or attested before me this _18th_ day of _January_ , 2018 by

TOM LANDWEHR, Commissioner of the Minnesota Department of Natural Resources.

Patricia Rae Blom
Notary Public

7

MISSISSIPPI

E. Ethelbert Miller

"Does William Faulkner Ever Sleep?" is a found poem. I discovered the words when I went to the "Oxford Bookstore" website. I added the title since the store isn't far from Faulkner's home in Oxford, Mississippi.

When I think of Mississippi, I think of Square Books in Oxford, Mississippi. It's one of the best independent bookstores in the country. Its existence and beauty almost overshadows the historical darkness once associated with "Ole Miss" and James Meredith's decision to integrate the college.

DOES WILLIAM FAULKNER EVER SLEEP?

Oxford Bookstore

We are revamping our website

We will be back soon

MISSOURI

Dorothea Lasky

"I felt like a complete outsider, the only one of my kind. So I just went off by myself, out in the world, to walk in the pastures and be with the animals. I was lonely, but I didn't dwell on it. I just said, 'Okay,' and I became accustomed to it, I guess. I had my own other thing going, my own world. And that was the beginning for me. I didn't have anybody, really, no foundation in life, so I had to make my own way. Always. From the start. I had to go out in the world and become strong, to discover my mission in life."

— Tina Turner's memories of childhood, taken from *I, Tina*, HarperCollins Publishers, 1986

Growing up in St. Louis, I would sometimes walk in The Loop and see the stars on the Walk of Fame. My father had grown up around there. My family's shoe store, called Lasky Shoes, had been in the Loop for a great deal of the 20th century, but was torn down at some point when I was a little girl. When I went to college, I lived for two years on Washington Avenue, right off the main drag. I knew Tina Turner's star very well. I've always loved her. Although our hearts do not feel exactly the same, I have a feeling of great familiarity when I hear her songs. *She is my Missouri Goddess.*

MONTANA

Prageeta Sharma

I happened upon this poster tacked onto the bulletin board listing spring events in Eck Hall near the English department in the Liberal Arts building at the University of Montana, where I work. I walk down this corridor and by this board nearly every day I'm on campus and I rarely see posters with brown and black faces on it. I am very proud that we hosted this evening with Mayor Collins, and this poster fills me with a particular, heartfelt joy that Montana can recognize and celebrate the true and exuberant leadership we have among us. For more information about Mayor Collins, please see carnegie.org /awards/honoree/wilmot-collins.

"Wilmot Collins (born October 15, 1963) is a Liberian-born American politician and the current mayor of Helena, Montana.[1] He defeated four-term incumbent mayor James E. Smith in the 2017 mayoral election on November 7, 2017 with 51% of the vote. This victory made him the first black person to be elected the mayor of any city in the history of Montana since statehood.[2] In 1873, pre-statehood Montana elected the first black mayor of any city in the territory of Montana with the election of E. T. Johnson, a black barber from Washington, D.C. Johnson's victory occurred before Montana had become a state or Helena had been officially incorporated as a city. Collins fled his native Liberia for Helena in 1994, as a refugee from the First Liberian Civil War.[5] He had petitioned for refugee status to join his wife, who had moved to Montana two years before he did.[3] He subsequently became a United States citizen, and worked for the Montana Department of Health and Human Services, specializing in child protection.[2] For two decades, he has been a member of the United States Navy Reserve. Collins has two children with his wife, their daughter, Jaymie and their son, Bliss." — Wikipedia

An Evening With Mayor

WILMOT

COLLINS

Montana's First
Black Mayor

THURSDAY APRIL 26th

University Center Theater
DOORS OPEN AT 5:00 pm
EVENT BEGINS AT 5:30 pm

FREE AND OPEN TO THE PUBLIC

NEBRASKA

Matt Mason

I've never seen anything like this. A midday sunset with half the state as well as people from surrounding states squeezed into a pencil-thin line across a map of Nebraska, traffic jams on small highways and county roads. And I took a million photos.
They all stank. Captured nothing like what I saw. So when I saw Tim Guthrie's photo, I was grateful, as this is actually what I saw that day.

Thanks, Tim.

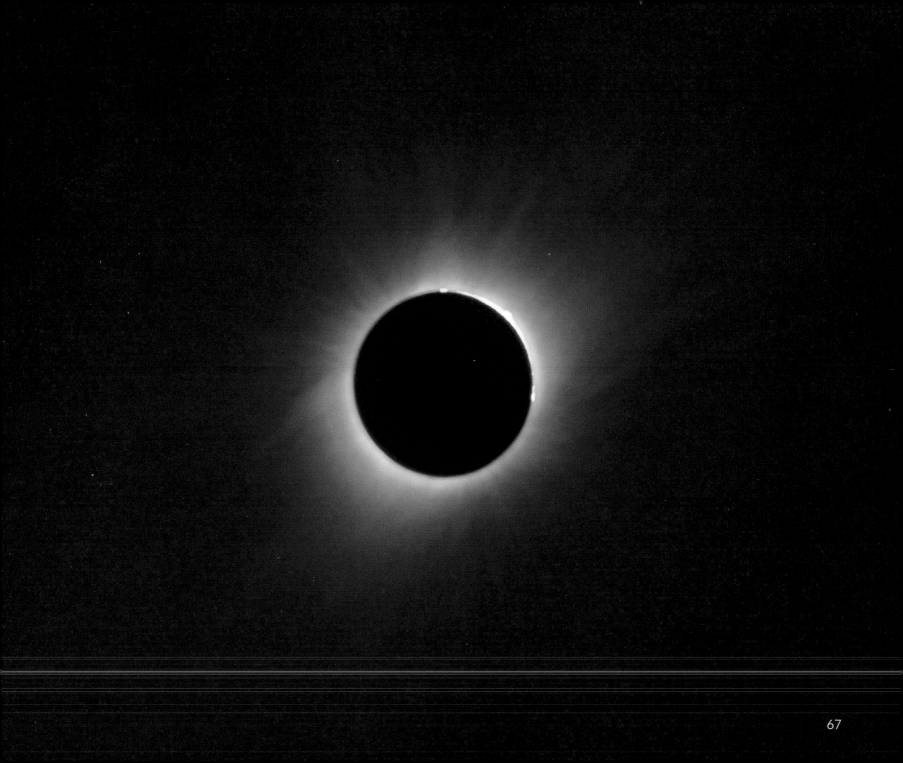

NEVADA

Vogue Robinson

"I think it pisses God off if you walk by the color purple in a field somewhere and don't notice it. People think pleasing God is all God cares about. But any fool living in the world can see it always trying to please us back."

— Alice Walker, *The Color Purple*

Ashamedly, I took this photograph at a red light. As my camera flashed the light turned green, giving the photo more meaning. It was intended as a "pick-me-up" for my friend, Jenise, on the day before her birthday. She constantly inspires me. I hoped this image would inspire her.

People spend a lot of time talking about the neon lights in Las Vegas as they fly into the city at night. The real light show has always been the Vegas sky. The sun rises and falls with splendor here. The kind of glory that requires attention. I think it pisses God off if you never look up at the Vegas sky.

It is also your loss.

Photo by Vogue Robinson

NEW HAMPSHIRE

Kate Greenstreet

I love the way snow, as it accumulates, creates something like a clean slate. But more beautiful to me are the marks we make in that blankness—footprints and tire tracks, the wide scrapes of ploughs, the stubborn progress of shovels—the shapes and patterns of our movement through time and bad weather.

Photo by Kate Greenstreet

NEW JERSEY

Cortney Lamar Charleston

Blue. Wave.

I'm a commuter, an underground railroad rider with a station situated a smooth four blocks from my shoebox apartment, adjacent from a Dunkin' Donuts. My head has been down so often I neglected the mural above the corporate coffeehouse: a mighty wave of blues rolling past Lady Liberty, who lives closer to this city than the more famous one.

I'm thinking forward to November, praying for a blue wave to wash the fascists out. To work and from, every shameful day now, I take in this mural from a different angle. Maybe that act, of looking aslant, is all that hope is. I lean into it, away from what devastates me.

The Jersey City Wave, a mural by Shepard Fairey
Photo by Cortney Lamar Charleston

NEW MEXICO

Arthur Sze

From December 4–7, 2018, the Santa Fe Council on International Relations staged the inaugural Journalism on Fire, where essential connections between journalism and democracy were explored. I attended the opening convocation, where Santa Fe mayor Alan Webber delivered a beautiful welcoming speech. I have excerpted the second half, which articulates a call to action. The launched conference went on for several days to great success, and I have included the Council on International Relations' response.

Journalism
Under Fire
are we free without a free press?

From Santa Fe Mayor Alan Webber's Welcoming Speech

- You know how to tell a story that captures the imagination of the world. Will you tell your powerful stories to the world, coming out of this gathering?

- Will you send a Santa Fe Statement—a journalistic manifesto—out to the world to memorialize this moment? Will you craft a bold statement of principle during this time in Santa Fe—a proclamation that will seize this moment and turn it into a declaration of unyielding commitment to the principles of a free press?

- As a union of fearless journalists, what will you band together to accomplish? Is there a global "NATO Alliance" of journalists that you will announce coming out of this meeting—a pronouncement that, from this time forward, an attack on one is an attack on all? Will you leave Santa Fe having formed a new united front, re-committed to the cause of journalistic justice, an enduring resistance to the ugly faces of fascism, dictatorship, censorship, and suppression, wherever they may rise up?

- In the end, the truth will endure, freedom will triumph, and free voices will rise to be heard—all over the world—***if we are willing to take on this fight***. It is not your fight alone—we are here to enlist in the cause as well. That is the pledge we make to you.

- Now, let us observe a moment of silence for the ***48 journalists who have been killed for doing their jobs just this year, for the 262 journalists*** who have been imprisoned since 2017, and for every journalist who has suffered as a martyr in years past to bring us the truth.

*

A moment of silence.

From the Sante Fe Statement on Journalism Under Fire

Hosted by the Santa Fe Council on International Relations and supported by prominent national and international partners, the event spotlighted ideas about, opinions, comments, and support for the following themes:

• Freedom of speech is a basic human right, and thus the role of journalism in pursuit of free speech must, by extension, be a core dimension of every society.

• Those individuals, groups, and nations with the greatest access to truth have the greatest capacity to contribute to their own liberty, prosperity, and security.

• Through its dedication to exploring and discovering the truth and holding power to account, professional journalism is indispensable to this endeavor and is a universal public good.

• Deliberate falsification and misinformation aid and abet those individuals or groups that seek to extract unfair economic or political advantage.

• All forms of persecution against journalists pursuing their professional duties is a violation of the fundamental human right of free expression.

• Diversity within journalism—with specific attention to women and ethnic minorities—is crucial to ensuring human rights and incorporating the perspectives, needs, and realities of all constituents.

Among the ways that participants suggested action on these themes were:

• Defending the independence of journalists in their pursuit of the truth in countries and societies across the globe.

• Condemning persecution or intimidation of journalists, and insisting that justice be brought against the perpetrators of abuses.

• Protesting misinformation perpetrated by media or leaders.

• Demanding that news media reflect the constituents they serve, through diverse newsrooms featuring a representative array of voices.

• Financially supporting independent, professional journalists, media, and journalism advocacy organizations in all possible ways, from the local to the national and international levels.

• Supporting media literacy to ensure that elementary, secondary, and post- secondary education cultivates students who can think critically.

• Support the election of officials who recognize freedom of speech as a basic human right, who understand the essential role journalism plays in self-determination and self-government, and who support and defend journalism and journalists.

Further, the Santa Fe Council on International Relations committed itself to staging a follow-up event on many of these themes in 2019.

NEW YORK

Jennifer Firestone

When Ava was eleven, she wrote this poem after beginning to independently ride the NYC subway to her middle school. This poem does not simply wax poetic over a romantic narrative of origin. Instead, the speaker in "I Am From" turns empathy and observation toward her surroundings and asks difficult questions about equity and suffering.
This poem is filled with humanity. It is also a love poem to her hometown, Brooklyn.

I AM FROM

by Ava Firestone-Morrill

I am from the window
People watching, observing
Awareness
Nature

I am from the paper
That clean white sheet to fullness
Finish
Completeness

I am from the beanbag
Snuggling
Letting me sink in
Becoming its sleepiness and
boredom with laziness combined

I am from the books
The stories
The poems
Taking me through adventure
after adventure

Going into other worlds
Other lives
Other people
Sucking me up, away from my
senses

From the weeping willows
From the Shakespeare
From the plays
From the music

From the writing
From the reading
From the dancing
The me is me

I am from losing yet to be gaining
Winning
From happiness to treachery
I am from a crack growing bigger
and bigger in the window pane

I am from a hurting heart to
rejoicing
I am from a roof, food, and water
containing me
All my needs met

I am from my dad next to the
microphone
Singing my heart out
Is this who I am?
I am from moving freely

From my mom
Words developing trickling and
tickling my tongue
Words turning into sentences
into paragraphs into books

I am from my friends
Good ones
True
I am from being myself
Being me

Teasing a mean soul
Not tolerated in me
I am from my brother
And sister
There for me
I am from my friends

Good ones
True
I am from being myself
Being me

From my hobbies and talents
I am from my individuality
Equality
I am from Brooklyn

But also from the birds chirping
and the grass zinging
Flowers budding
then opening
I am from the ivy growing on
the back fence

The nature
The freeness
Escaping for fresh air
To do those
cartwheels
Space not limited

"Brooklyn?" you may ask
The tall buildings
The crowdedness
The bubbling

I am from the diversity
I am from busyness
From rush hour
From the subway platform

To seeing the people begging for a
drop of kindness
Homeless
Just innocent people, troubled
I am from me struggling to
control my anger
of no one helping them

Keeping their heads up high
ignoring
As I am fortunate,
if in their place I would feel
hatred for those people ignoring
What can you say?

What can you do?
Do people have to suffer?
It is New York
I'm a city girl

But alas, everywhere I go
becoming a part of me, leaving
and taking a piece of me, while
others revolve around me
This is how my world works
This is where I am from

NORTH CAROLINA

Dorianne Laux

I was walking through my neighborhood in Five Points, Raleigh, NC, when I came across this flyer tacked to a telephone pole. How potently true, I thought, especially here where five roads come together in the middle of what used to be a very smal town. The tiny post office was built in the early 1900s. The Rialto Theater opened in 1942. Before it was renovated, it was the local A&P (1936) which sported pine floors, plastic walls, and a celotex ceiling before being converted. The railroad runs along one border of Five Points and freight trains stop at the old service station. The Norfolk Southern line carries food and supplies to 24 seaports, 10 river ports, and 9 Great Lake ports. The small bungalow-type houses are surrounded by old forest which hosts owls, hawks, an occasional falcon, and the very occasional bear. It's also home to the oldest inhabitants, the remaining Indigenous People of Raleigh: the Tuscarora, the Catawba, the Lumbee, and the Siouan Tribes. "We were a group that was intentionally wiped out and our culture erased, and we're still here," says Trey Roberts, a Haliwa-Saponi native. Recently, the Raleigh City Council approved changing the name of Aycock Street to Roanoke Park Drive, removing the name of the racist Charles Aycock to the name of the Roanoac Tribe, a Carolina Algonquian-speaking people whose territory comprised present-day Dare County, now the corner where this telephone pole stands. Here, where we sleep beneath the oldest mountain range in the United States which has been being worn down for centuries, home of the Black River and the Methuselah tree, a swamp cypress that took root in 364 A.D. Who's to say that everything doesn't happen, or hasn't happened, right here, in the middle of nowhere? I mean masses of people once banded together to build and pave five diagonal roads, which when seen from above create a starburst shape, our town the hub of this particular universe, each road leading to this very spot, then built a railroad to pass through it like a river of steam and steel, erected a post office to send letters from and to the people who lived in these wood-framed houses with brick fireplaces and mailboxes painted red, who got up from their couches and donned their fancy clothes, collected their hats and coats and walked down to the movie theater to see what in the world everyone else was doing with their miraculously accidental lives.

Photo by Dorianne Laux

NORTH DAKOTA

Denise K. Lajimodiere

The local high school was holding a poetry workshop and I came upon this poem outside the school. To the Native people the Dragonfly is a sacred creature, carrying the spirits of our ancestors to earth to visit us. When landing on you, moving their little feet, they are healing your spirit of all that is not good; they are the power of love made constant.

Photo by Denise K. Lajimodiere

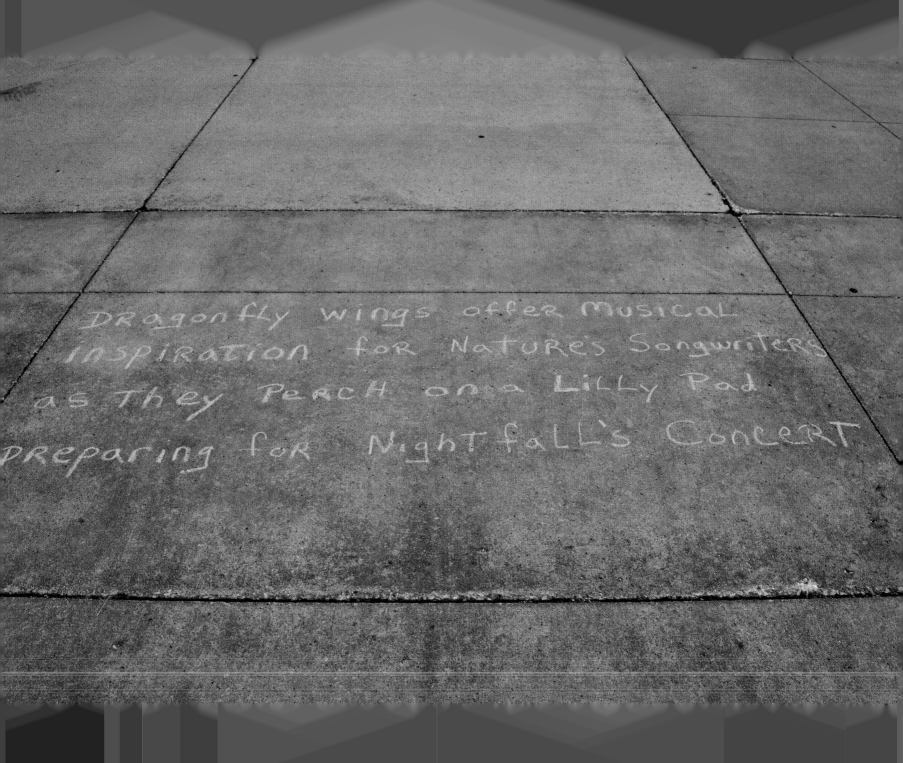

Dragonfly wings offer musical
inspiration for Nature's Songwriters
as They Perch on a Lilly Pad
preparing for Nightfall's Concert

OHIO

Amit Majmudar

Descending from the east into Cleveland's airport, our plane passed over the suburb where I grew up. My son took this picture. So many vulnerabilities in this one photograph: our houses that could at any moment be foreclosed or plummet in value; our plane with nothing bearing it up but faith and science and swiftness; and, in the upper right hand margin, a storm I hope isn't a metaphor for our American future. In the real world, at least, there was a happy ending. We landed safely, and the storm hit right after we got our daughter's car seat installed and shut the trunk on the last of the luggage, and we drove home to my parents, who live in the house where I grew up. There are tens of thousands, in this age of displacement, who are not so lucky. They are standing in the storm. I pray that they and their families, too, may land safely, and together, and get to shelter soon.

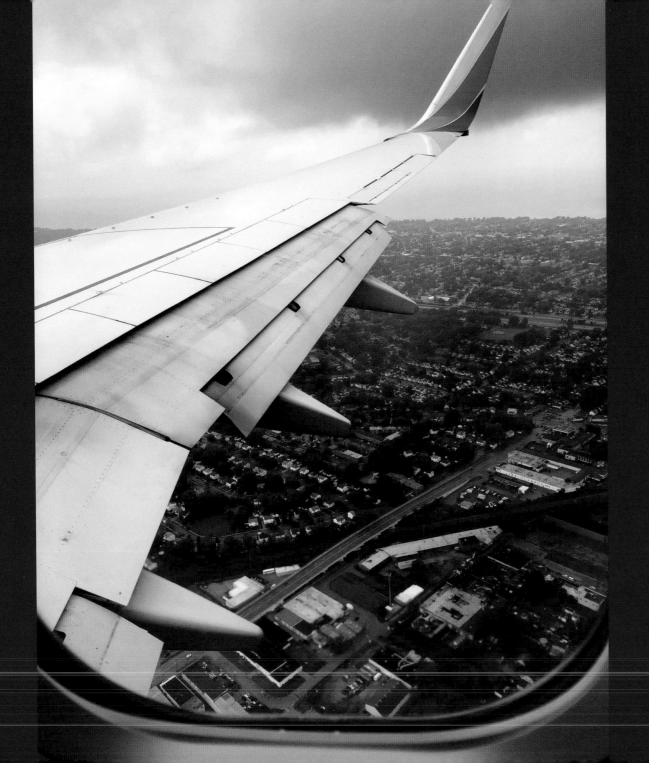

OKLAHOMA

Joy Harjo

Two years ago was the culmination of the first round of arts mentorships for young Muscogee Creek women in Oklahoma. Louisa Harjo, a high school artist, was paired with one of our most beloved artists, Dana Tiger. This mentorship program, "For Girls Becoming," was founded by Joy Harjo and is continuing its work through the Mvskoke Nation Youth Services. Dana's father was the famous artist Jerome Tiger. At the community feast, Louisa and Dana presented the work they had accomplished together. They have a special connection, which is visible in this photograph taken by my sister Margaret Barrows.

Photo by Margaret Barrows

OREGON

Douglas Manuel

The 1857 Oregon Constitution is ugly, but remembering the ugly, caustic, and vitriolic history of our country can be a beautiful process because reminiscing shows us the progress we've made, motivates us to keep going. Lately, it feels like much progress has been lost. Justice and freedom can dissolve as easy as the weather changes, and the political weather has indeed changed, so I remember us being uglier before, to evoke progress, to keep going.

SELECTIONS FROM THE 1857 OREGON CONSTITUTION

Section No.6

No Negro, Chinaman, or Mulatto shall have the right of suffrage.-

Section No. 2

Each elector who offers to vote upon this constitution shall be asked by the judges of election this question: Do you vote for the constitution? Yes or No. And also this question. Do you vote for slavery in Oregon? Yes or No. And also this question. Do you vote for the free Negroes in Oregon? Yes or No. And in the poll books shall be columns headed respectably. "Constitution, yes." "Constitution, no." "Free Negroes, yes." "Free Negroes, no." "Slavery, yes." "Slavery, no." And if a majority of all the votes given for, and against free Negroes, shall be given against free Negroes, then the following section shall be added to the Bill of Rights, and shall be part of this constitution: "Sec.–No free Negro, or Mulatto, not residing in this state at the time of the adoption of this constitution, shall come, reside, or be within this state, or hold any real estate, or make any contracts, or maintain any suit therein; an the Legislative Assembly shall provide by penal laws, for the removal, by public officers, of all such Negroes, and Mulattos, and for their effectual exclusion from the state, and for the punishment of persons who shall bring them into the state, or employ, or harbor them."- (The free Negro clause was repealed, November 3, 1926, infra. It was Section 35 of article I.)

31.-

White foreigners who are, or may hereafter become residents of this State shall enjoy the same rights in respect to the possession, enjoyment, and descent of property as native born citizens. And the Legislative Assembly shall have the power to restrain, and regulate the immigration to this State of persons not qualified to become Citizens of the United States.-

PENNSYLVANIA

Raquel Salas Rivera

This photograph was taken by one of my closest friends, Karenina Angleró, who relocated to Philadelphia after Hurricane María. It was taken at the launch of the *We (Too) Are Philly* summer festival I've been organizing since I became Poet Laureate. It shows the Puerto Rican poet Denice Frohman and myself listening to one of the many performers that participated in a night celebrating Black and Brown joy. Moments like these are why I love Philly.

Philadelphia, 2018

Photo by Karenina Angleró, 2018

RHODE ISLAND

Sawako Nakayasu

On my way to work one day, I found this plaque memorializing the great soprano Sissieretta Jones, at the site of her former home in Providence. I had read about her in *Olio* by Tyehimba Jess, in which he quotes from a WPA interview: *She'd turn all your moments inside out. Seemed like sometimes she'd take a whole year's worth of seasons and pour it into one moan, standin up there with her mouth swallowing up everyone's sorrow one note at a time.* Since 1933, Jones had been buried in an unmarked grave in Grace Episcopal Church Cemetery in Providence. Through the efforts of her biographer, Maureen Lee, and Ray Rickman, executive director of Stages of Freedom, a local nonprofit bookstore supporting swim lessons for inner-city youth, she received her headstone on June 9, 2018.

Photo by Sawako Nakayasu

SISSIERETTA JONES
"The Greatest Singer of Her Race"
1868~1933

Matilda Sissieretta Joyner Jones,
the internationally celebrated soprano
known as "Black Patti," lived near this
site at 7 Wheaton Street until her passing
on June 24, 1933.

With 17 medals and a diamond tiara
bestowed upon her, she was the highest paid
performer of her race and the first African
American woman to appear at Carnegie Hall.
For 28 years she toured the world, singing
for 75,000 at Madison Square Garden,
four U.S. presidents, the German Kaiser,
and British Royalty.

She is buried at
Grace Church Cemetery, Providence.

ERECTED BY THE RHODE ISLAND BLACK HERITAGE SOCIETY

SOUTH CAROLINA

Marcus Amaker

This is a photo of an unfinished mural in Charleston, SC. It's in an area that has seen a lot of growth. When it was completed, artist Nysa Hicks asked people to write their response and reaction to the phrase "Free me from . . ." Those responses are now peppered all over the wall. For a city that has been through two racially charged massacres since 2015, it's important that we lean on art to open us up to conversation and growth. That's what this mural represents to me—a beautiful chance to move forward.

Photo by Marcus Amaker

SOUTH DAKOTA

Lee Ann Roripaugh

In downtown Vermillion, South Dakota, adjacent to City Hall, I'm always drawn to this graffiti on concrete that reads, "It's not you. It's me." Is it the androgynous quality of the face without hair? The chunky white bangles? Or the wig-like golden halo around the head? While the text mocks the clichéd breakup line, I find it's an important reminder that other people's actions are about them and not me.

Photo by Lee Ann Roripaugh

TENNESSEE

Ama Codjoe

My twin cousins celebrated their first birthday in Memphis, Tennessee, on St. Patrick's Day. And though we aren't Irish, their parents sported bright green shirts that read: *Lucky*. Fifty years after Dr. King's assassination on the balcony of the Lorraine Hotel, there is still a need to proclaim "I Am a Man." And yet, the children are eager for cake. And yet, sometimes we feel our blessings like a crown of flowers on our heads.

Photo provided by Ama Codjoe

TEXAS

Ching-In Chen

On a cross-country road trip in and out of Texas, my partner Cassie Mira started capturing lightning near El Paso, Texas while I was driving. Much of my time in Texas is spent on the drive. There are moments when I'm startled out of my auto-pilot, when I look up at the chameleon sky—sometimes ominous, sometimes a rumble—and the surprise is full of pleasure.

Photo from *After El Paso* by Cassie Mira

UTAH

Craig Dworkin

An old totalitarian trick: provoke discord to consolidate support for policed control. But the inverse also occurs: autocratic rule provokes exuberant and unexpected resistance—different languages, but all speaking to the same thing. Social wrongs don't just harm their most obvious and immediate victims, but everyone in the system—all of whom are dancing, discordantly, together.

Language from Barack Obama's presidential proclamation establishing the Bears Ears National Monument, as quoted by Angelo Baca and Willi Grayeyes

RISING AND DANCING

Rising from the center of the southeastern Utah landscape and visible from every direction are twin buttes so distinctive that in each of the native languages of the region their name is the same: Hoon'Naqvut, Shash Jáa, Kwiyagatu Nukavachi, Ansh An Lashokdiwe, or "Bears Ears."

Protecting Bears Ears is not just about healing for the land and Native people. It's for our adversaries to be healed, too. I truly believe we can all come out dancing together.

VERMONT

Camille Guthrie

When I moved to rural Vermont eleven years ago, I was astonished to find myself living in a house with a pond and a barn—for far less than the small rental in Brooklyn I left. For a long time I felt lonely, scared of catamounts, anxious about guns. Now I love the lilacs, the bears who break open my garden shed, and my friends who raise their own sheep—although the winter still lingers too long. At the moment, we are staying in place. Friends are expanding their gardens, baking bread, sewing masks, going birding, and protesting injustice and racism however they can. Our poet laureate, Mary Ruefle, plans to handwrite poems to 1,000 recipients chosen randomly from the state phone book for the Poet Laureate Fellowship program from the Academy of American Poets—beautiful!

vermontbiz.com/people/may/mary-ruefle-named-academy-american-poets-laureate-fellow

Mary Ruefle named Academy of American Poets Laureate Fellow

Tweet Like 6

Thu, 05/28/2020 - 1:30pm -- Denise Sortor

There are the poets laureate of cities, counties, and states, and then there are the poets laureate fellows of the American Academy of Poets. The Academy launched the Poets Laureate Fellowship program in 2019 to honor poets appointed to civil positions and enable them to carry out exceptional, impactful work in their communities. In 2020, only 23 poets received the honor, and Vermont's own Poet Laureate Mary Ruefle is one of them.

Mary Ruefle is the author of many books of poetry, including *Dunce* (Wave Books, 2019), finalist for the 2020 Pulitzer Prize and longlisted for the 2019 National Book Award in Poetry. She is the recipient of a Guggenheim Fellowship, a National Endowment for the Arts Fellowship, and a Whiting Award. Ruefle is the Poet Laureate of Vermont, where she lives in Bennington and taught for over twenty years in the MFA program at Vermont College. In collaboration with the Vermont Arts Council, Ruefle will personally mail out handwritten poems written by other poets to 1,000 residents of Vermont, randomly chosen from the phonebook.

Mary spoke with us following the announcement of her fellowship, offering this statement:

"I was thrilled to receive the grant, both for myself and the state. And the timing couldn't have been better—I support myself by traveling around the country and giving readings and talks, and my entire 2020 itinerary was canceled. The grant more than made up for the loss, and I did not have to apply for self-unemployment with the state, which makes those precious funds available to others, all of whom, I am sure, are more deserving.

"Arts organizations, like the Arts Council, are absolutely essential at all times, and even more so in times like these. I believe the arts are an essential business; look at it this way—we are not literally saving lives, but do you want to survive a pandemic only to live in a world without art? And as all things are ultimately connected, we could say the same thing about nature.

"I actually began mailing out poems locally before I got the grant, but receiving the grant will enable me to reach my goal of 1,000 poems. I know most will end up in the trash, but I hope 10% of them will reach people whose day will be made a little brighter, richer, deeper.

"And lastly, I want to publicly thank Governor Scott for the terrific job he has done with unfailing energy and courage; we were so lucky to have him in office at this embattled time."

The poet laureate serves as Vermont's ambassador for the art of poetry and is called upon to participate in official ceremonies and readings within Vermont and nationally. This is a four-year honorary position, appointed by the governor based on the recommendation of a distinguished panel of judges. Vermont's first Poet Laureate, Robert Frost, was appointed in 1961. In 1988, Governor Madeline Kunin re-established the position. Since 1988, Sydney Lea, Ruth Stone, Grace Paley, Ellen Bryant Voigt, Louise Glück, Galway Kinnell and Chard deNiord have held the post.

About the Vermont Arts Council

The Vermont Arts Council envisions a Vermont where all people have access to the arts and creativity in their lives, education, and communities. Engagement with the arts transforms individuals, connects us more deeply to each other, energizes the economy, and sustains the vibrant cultural landscape that makes Vermont a great place to live. Since 1965, the Council has been the state's primary provider of funding, advocacy, and information for the arts in Vermont. Learn more at vermontartscouncil.org

Photo credit: Shawn Sullivan

Related Company:
Vermont Arts Council

VIRGINIA

giovanni singleton

As a kid, I sometimes arrived at Mt. Sinai Baptist Church, located less than half a mile from where Patrick Henry famously proclaimed, "Give Me Liberty or Give Me Death," with a sore butt for not wanting to wake up early for morning service. Aunt Lily Mae was the church clerk, so we were never late. Sometimes the choir would sing *This little light of mine/I'm gonna let it shine, let it shine/Everywhere I go* . . . a much needed balm that called in the day's early light which reshaped my vision as it filtered through panes of glass stained sea green and sunflower. Now, many years later, I sometimes wonder if how we see ourselves, and the world around us, might be colored by the lens through which we decide to look, revealing a little light shining, shining everywhere we go . . .

Photo by giovanni singleton

WASHINGTON

Sally and Sam Green

Our granddaughter discovered these moss-covered shoes just off a trail on the tiny island where she lives. We think they are not only sculpturally beautiful, but also an unintentional *memento mori*, how transient we are. New, they would look out of place; now they have come home, visually and literally, as food for moss. We make a great shouting as a people, but there is an interior place in us, something like Ciardi's "haunted silence."

Photo by Cora Green

WASHINGTON, D.C.

Sarah Anne Cox

Something Beautiful: Washington D.C., The Funk Parade

I wanted to select something that would reflect the more permanent community of D.C. Many in D.C. and the surrounding area live there for a few years or decades (like myself) before moving elsewhere, home or another temporary home. The Funk Parade that began nine years ago was a grassroots, neighborhood event that marched from the Lincoln to the Howard Theatre, down U Street. It's a celebration of a diverse community, distinctly African American but also home to Caribbean and Ethiopian immigrant communities. I include the Funk Parade stamp as a beautiful object.

funkparade.com

WEST VIRGINIA

Marc Harshman

On February 22nd, 2018, a nine-day, state-wide—all fifty-five WV counties—teachers' strike began, a strike that included service personnel, as well. It was marked by the worst kind of politicking orchestrated by an overwhelmingly Republican state legislature. West Virginia teachers have for many years drawn one of the lowest average salaries of any teachers in the United States. Some teachers live "paycheck to paycheck" and have to have a second job to make ends meet. Although threatened with legal action by the state Attorney General, the teachers remained united and eventually won their demand for better pay and more secure insurance coverage which has positive implications for all state employees. At the time of this writing, teachers across Oklahoma had been considering a similar strike for April. Some pundits believe this heroic stand by the teachers in conservative West Virginia may have lit a flame that will spread to other unions across the nation.

THE BEAUTY OF RESISTANCE

Assembled on the occasion of the West Virginia Teachers' Strike, 3.22–4.7, 2018.

Teacher and student posters are shown in bold type and a variety of literary and historical quotations, shown in italics, alternate with these.

Fifty-five United!

Education is the most powerful weapon which you can use to change the world.

— Nelson Mandela

I would rather be teaching!

Intelligence plus character—that is the goal of true education.

— Martin Luther King Jr.

Dear students " . . . *because you're mine, I walk the line.*"

Kids . . . don't remember what you try to teach them. They remember what you are.

— Jim Henson, *It's Not Easy Being Green: And Other Things to Consider*

Teachers: WV's Biggest Export!

If you think education is expensive, try ignorance.

— Robert Orben

"I get paid too much . . ." said <u>no</u> teacher <u>ever</u>.

Teaching is not a lost art, but the regard for it is a lost tradition.

— Jacques Barzun

My second job bought this sign!

Human history becomes more and more a race between education and catastrophe.

— H.G. Wells

Give us some [of the] fracking money!

You can't stop a teacher when they want to do something. They just do it.

— J.D. Salinger, *The Catcher in the Rye*

Will teach for insurance. Insurance should not cost a living wage.

"Wrote my way out of the hood . . . thought my way out of poverty! Don't tell me that knowledge isn't power. Education changes everything."

— Brandi L. Bates

Protect us, not guns!

With guns you can kill terrorists, with education you can kill terrorism.

— Malala Yousafzai

THE BEAUTY OF RESISTANCE, P. 2

If teachers are last, you can't put students first!

He who opens a school door, closes a prison.

— Victor Hugo

No more lip service for this speech teacher.

It is very nearly impossible to become an educated person in a country so distrustful of the independent mind.

— James Baldwin

This would never happen at Hogwarts.

The educated differ from the uneducated as much as the living differ from the dead.

— Aristotle

We wish the state [politicians] loved us like we love our students.

The main hope of a nation lies in the proper education of its youth.

— Erasmus

When we stand up for ourselves, we stand up for our students.

The secret of education lies in respecting the pupil.

— Ralph Waldo Emerson

Why are our teachers leaving?

How is it that little children are so intelligent and men so stupid? It must be education that does it.

— Alexandre Dumas

Our legislators are walking out on us! Our teachers are standing up for us!

All of life is a constant education.

— Eleanor Roosevelt, *The Wisdom of Eleanor Roosevelt*

Our parents understand . . . . So why don't you?

Education is our passport to the future, for tomorrow belongs to the people who prepare for it today.

— Malcolm X

THE BEAUTY OF RESISTANCE, P. 3

WV preschool teachers 6th best in nation–49th in pay!

When you study great teachers . . . you will learn much more from their caring and hard work than from their style.

— William Glasser

$140 million [in WV] corporate tax breaks . . . give us break!

In the first place God made idiots. This was for practice. Then he made school boards. [here read certain state legislators]

— Mark Twain, *Following the Equator: A Journey Around the World*

I teach my students to stand up for themselves: here's my real life example!

Education is not the filling of a pail, but the lighting of a fire.

— W.B. Yeats

This was once illegal too! (from poster with picture of Rosa Parks sitting at front of bus—this picture chosen after WV attorney general asserts the strike is illegal)

The learning process is something you can incite, literally incite, like a riot.

— Audre Lorde

This once sleeping giant has awakened and will be voting . . .

Democracy cannot succeed unless those who express their choice are prepared to choose wisely. The real safeguard of democracy, therefore, is education.

— Franklin D. Roosevelt

West Virginia Teachers lead the way: SPREAD the STRIKE . . .

The great aim of education is not knowledge but action.

— Herbert Spencer

These are the faces of democracy.

This is . . . democracy!

WISCONSIN

Oliver Baez Bendorf

Wisconsin gets very bleak over the long winter, but it is also beautiful. One of the most incredible parts is that all the lakes and ponds freeze over to ice, and the ice fills with fishing huts, also known as bobhouses or ice shanties. Idiosyncratic and ephemeral, these shelters spring up on frozen water, and are towed away before the ice turns to slush, and then water, again.

"Let me see what stories I can tell you from way out here in Wisconsin . . . Everybody is going out on the ice on the lake to fish. They take little huts along to sit in while their lines and hooks hang outside, down through the holes in the ice. The huts are heated and there the people sit and play cards. Someday I'll get tired of trying to write radio scripts and jump into my waste basket which I'll have on skids and I'll skedoodle out onto the lake."

— Lorine Niedecker, in a letter to Paul Zukofsky dated February 7, 1952

Photo by Oliver Baez Bendorf

Ice fishing hut at Devil's Lake State Park, Baraboo, Wisconsin, January 14, 2018

WYOMING

David Romtvedt

Asked about contributing to this anthology, I thought of what gives me joy and hope. Maybe something in Basque, a language that has been under fire for thousands of years and yet is still alive and vibrant. Marrying into a Wyoming Basque family, I've learned this language that is different from any I've encountered. Ederra den hizkuntza—beautiful in its own right and as an element of human diversity. I thought too about sending a poem—so many poets have offered me an entry into beauty.

In the end, I decided on a song—Manhã de Carnaval (Carnival Morning). Written for the Brazilian film *Black Orpheus* by Luiz Bonfa with lyrics by Antonio Maria, it has been recorded many times. It's sung here by my daughter

Caitlin Belem Romtvedt with the band Maracujá playing at Empty Sea Studios in Seattle, Washington. There is the tragic story of Eurydice and Orpheus, the sonic beauty of the song, and the fact of its being sung by my daughter whose birth brought a second life to my own. Through my daughter, I was given the opportunity to grow in ways I'd never imagined. The heartless rulers of the Underworld were wrong—there are second chances.

Every Carnival season offers opportunity. When we sing this song, the universal is made personal and individual— the beauty of the morning, of tomorrow, of what is possible even in the face of what is lost, feelings that come from our deepest relationships with one another. It's beautiful.

While the anthology can't include recordings, please scan the QR code to the right or visit: youtube.com/watch?v=0amGL0X0YVI.

Here are the lyrics as sung by Caitlin with my rather clunky translation:

MANHÃ DE CARNAVAL / CARNIVAL MORNING

Manhã tão bonita manhã
Na vida uma nova canção
Cantando so teus olhos
Teu riso, tuas mãos
Pois ha de haver um dia em que viras

Das cordas de meu violão
Que só teu amor procurou
Vem uma voz
falar dos beijos perdidos
Nos labios teus

Canta o meu coração
Alegria voltou
Tão feliz a manhã deste amor.

Morning, such a beautiful morning,
in life, a new song
singing only your eyes,
your laugh, your hands,
because there must be a day
on which you will come.

From the strings of my guitar
comes a voice
brought solely by your love,
a voice speaking of lost kisses,
lost on your lips.

My heart sings
happiness returned,
how happy the morning
of this love.

BIOGRAPHICAL STATEMENTS

ABOUT THE POETS

Listed Alphabetically by Location

Alabama

Jacqueline Allen Trimble is a Cave Canem Fellow and an Alabama State Council on the Arts Literary Fellow. Her poetry has appeared in *The Louisville Review*, *The Offing*, *Poet Lore*, the anthology *The Night's Magician* and other publications. Her essay "A Woman Explains How Learning Poetry is Poetry and Not Magic Made Her a Poet" appears in *Southern Writers on Writing*, an anthology of contemporary Southern writers. Published by NewSouth Books, *American Happiness*, her debut poetry collection, won the 2016 Balcones Poetry Prize. Jennifer Horne, poet laureate of Alabama, wrote about the collection, "Her grace is in the anger distilled to the bitter draft you savor as it bites," and Honorée Fanonne Jeffers, author of *The Age of Phillis*, said, "I longed for her kind of poetry, these cut-to-the-flesh poems, this verse that sings the old time religion of difficult truths with new courage and utter sister-beauty." Trimble recently wrote five episodes for *Die Testament*, a South African soap opera that streamed on Netwerk24, and is currently at work on a number of television projects. She is Professor of English and chairs the Department of Languages and Literatures at Alabama State University.

Joseph D. Trimble II lives and works in Montgomery, Alabama, where he studies graphic design. He primarily photographs architecture.

Alaska

X'unei Lance Twitchell is an Associate Professor of Alaska Native Languages at the University of Alaska Southeast and has been teaching Lingít, the Tlingit language, since 2004. He is also a multimedia artist who owns and operates a company called Troubled Raven. X'unei earned a Ph.D. in Hawaiian and Indigenous Language and Cultural Revitalization from Ka Haka 'Ula O Ke'elikōlani College of Hawaiian Language at the University of Hawai'i at Hilo. His studies are in creating safe language acquisition spaces and achieving revitalization through counter-hegemonic transformation, which means a rejection of external definitions and fragmentation and a promotion of the thought world of the ancestors of language movements. In 2013, he started working with Representative Jonathan Kreiss-Tomkins and a team of language advocates across the state to create and pass a bill that made Alaska Native languages the co-official languages of the state of Alaska. He is a multimedia artist and lives with his wife and three children in Juneau, Alaska.

Sāmoa ʻi Sasaʻe/American Samoa

Dan Taulapapa McMullin is a poet, painter, filmmaker, and conceptual artist from American Samoa. His collection of poems *Coconut Milk* was on the American Library Association's Ten Best LGBT Books of the Year List. His work has shown at the Metropolitan Museum, United Nations, Bishop Museum, De Young Museum, Auckland Art Gallery, and Musée du quai Branly. His most recent book is *Samoan Queer Lives*, co-edited with Yuki Kihara. His art appropriation film on tiki kitsch, *100 Tikis*, has screened internationally. He is working on a novel and lives in Hudson, New York, with his partner Stephen and a schnoodle named Roby. More on Taulapapa's work can be seen at taulapapa.com.

Sia Figiel is an award-winning novelist, performance-poet, storyteller and translator from Samoa.

Benjamin Garcia is a documentary filmmaker and photographer from the San Francisco Bay Area. His documentary work focuses on topics of race and culture, climate change, the criminal justice system, post-colonial perspectives, and historical American relationships. Influenced by his mixed background as a Black/Samoan/Ecuadorian-American filmmaker, he utilizes his passion and art to create impactful stories that inspire.

Benjamin is currently working on his debut feature film, *Farming For Sovereignty*, which follows a struggling island farmer as he strives to bring back ancient traditions of sustainability as the effects of climate change are actively disrupting modern life in American Samoa. Benjamin's Work: sinafilms.com

Arizona

Felicia Zamora's poetry books include *I Always Carry My Bones*, 2020 Iowa Poetry Prize winner (University of Iowa Press, 2021); *Quotient* (forthcoming, Tinderbox Editions); *Body of Render*, Benjamin Saltman Award winner (2020); and *Of Form & Gather*, Andrés Montoya Poetry Prize winner. She won the 2020 C.P. Cavafy Prize from Poetry International, the Wabash Prize for Poetry, and the Tomaž Šalamun Prize. Her poems appear in *American Poetry Review*, *Boston Review*, *Georgia Review*, *Guernica*, *Orion*, *Poetry*, *The Nation*, and others. She is an assistant professor of poetry at the University of Cincinnati and associate poetry editor for the *Colorado Review*.

Tonissa Saul is a writer and photographer from Arizona. She is the managing editor for *Bodega Magazine* and an editor for rinky dink press. Her work has appeared in *Write On*, *Downtown*, *The Comstock Review* and the anthology *Miles to Go, Promises to Keep Volume II*. Additionally, her artwork has appeared on the covers of rinky dink press collections.

Arkansas

Dana Teen Lomax's projects often involve collaboration in a variety of media including poetry, film, and performance. She has published extensively and uses both her writing and teaching to better understand the world. A fourth-generation Californian, Dana's people on her mom's side are from Lamar, Arkansas. Dana's mother, maternal grandparents, and great-grandparents are buried in a family plot in the Lamar Cemetery. Raised on collard greens, sweet tea, fried okra, and peach cobbler, Dana Teen Lomax misses Johnson County and the people from there who taught her how to love.

California

Jaime Cortez is a Northern California writer and visual artist. He has exhibited his art across the San Francisco Bay Area in venues that include the Oakland Museum of California, the Berkeley Art Museum, Yerba Buena Center for the Arts, Southern Exposure, and Galería de la Raza. His first short story collection will be published by Grove Atlantic Press in the summer of 2021. Jaime's work can be seen at jaimecortez.org.

Thad H. Austin was raised in the California coastal town of Watsonville in Pajaro Valley, attending public school through high school. In 1983, Austin moved to Pasadena CA, studying fine art and cinema briefly before moving to San Francisco to earn a degree in Cinema and a masters in mathematics education. He has taught public school in San Francisco since 1987 while privately painting in several mediums including acrylic and watercolor. Bio photo by Rothanak Park-Austin.

Colorado

Jovan Mays is the emeritus Poet Laureate of Aurora, Colorado, a National Poetry Slam Champion, and the Youth Voice Coordinator of Aurora Public Schools. Mays has worked with well over one million students through poetry outreach in his program Your Writing Counts. He is the author of three books: *Pride*, *The Great Box Escape*, and *This Is Your Song*. *The Pilgrimage*, *Button Poetry*, and *Write About Now* have published his work. He is a gradu-ate of Chadron State College, where he played football, wrestled, and earned a degree in Secondary History Education.

Connecticut

Rayon Lennon was born in rural Jamaica; he moved to New Haven County, Connecticut, U.S.A., when he was 13. He currently resides in New Haven, CT. He holds a B.A. in English with a concentration in Creative Writing from Southern Connecticut State University. He holds a master's degree in Social Work. His work has been published widely in various literary magazines, including *StepAway Magazine*, *Callaloo* and *Rattle*. His poems have won numerous poetry awards, including the 2017 Rattle Poetry Prize contest for his poem "Heard." His first book of poems, *Barrel Children*, was a finalist for the 2017 Connecticut Book Award for best poetry book.

Delaware

Gemelle John is a poet and educator. While at the University of Delaware, she served as vice president of the university's spoken word organization, where she had the privilege to work with poets including Andrea Gibson, Clint Smith, and Alixa and Naima of Climbing PoeTree. Her work has since been featured in *Cleaver Magazine*, *Public Pool*, *Beltway Quarterly* and *The News Journal*. She was a 2018 Emerging Artist Fellow with the Delaware Division of the Arts and has received fellowships from VONA, Juniper, The Sanctuary Poets, and the Delaware Writers' Retreat. She was a committee member and presenter at the 2018 and 2019 Wilmington Writers Conference. She currently works as a Spanish teacher in Wilmington and continues to write, publish, and teach poetry and language.

Florida

Nicole Brodsky's work has appeared in numerous literary journals, most recently in *Your Impossible Voice*. She has published two books of poetry—*Getting Word* (Fourteen Hills Press) and *Gestic* (a+bend press). And while she currently lives in the Keystone State, she is, of course, from the Sunshine State.

Georgia

Jericho Brown is the recipient of a Whiting Writers' Award and fellowships from the John Simon Guggenheim Foundation, the Radcliffe Institute for Advanced Study at Harvard University, and the National Endowment for the Arts. Brown's first book, *Please* (2008), won the American Book Award. His second book, *The New Testament* (2014), won the Anisfield-Wolf Book Award and was named one of the best of the year by *Library Journal*, *Coldfront*, and the Academy of American Poets. He is also the author of the collection *The Tradition* (2019), which was a finalist for the 2019 National Book Award and the winner of the 2020 Pulitzer Prize for Poetry. His poems have appeared in *Buzzfeed*, *The Nation*, *The New York Times*, *The New Yorker*, *The New Republic*, *Time*, and *The Pushcart Prize Anthology*, and several volumes of *The Best American Poetry* anthologies. He is an associate professor and the director of the Creative Writing Program at Emory University in Atlanta.

Guåhan/Guam

Evelyn San Miguel Flores (*Familian Kabesa yan Yaman*) is a CHamoru writer from the island of Guåhan. Swimming, late afternoon beach walks, and hiking feed her creativity. Her poetry and short stories have been published in local and international, print and online publications, including *Storyboard*, *Local Voices*, and *Not A Muse: A World Poetry Anthology*. She and another Pacific Island writer are the editors of *An Anthology of Indigenous Literatures from Micronesia*, the first collection of its kind, published in 2019 by University of Hawai'i Press. Evelyn worked closely with Rosa Salas Palomo, a nest-language speaker, on the CHamoru translation for this piece.

Rosa Salas Palomo has made CHamoru language preservation her calling. She has served as director of the Bilingual-Bicultural Education Program at the University of Guam and is currently coordinating a five-year million-dollar grant from the U.S. Office of Education, Office of English Language Acquisition.

Hawai'i

No'u Revilla is a queer 'Ōiwi poet, educator, and aloha 'āina. Born and raised on the island of Maui, she has performed throughout Hawai'i as well as in Canada, Papua New Guinea, and at the United Nations. Read her work in *Anomaly*, *Literary Hub*, *Poetry magazine*, and *Black Renaissance Noire*. Her second chapbook *Permission to Make Digging Sounds* was published in *Effigies III* in 2019. She is proud to have taught poetry at Pu'uhuluhulu University while standing with her lāhui to protect Maunakea.

Idaho

Janet Holmes is a poet and taught at Boise State University, where she directed and edited Ahsahta Press for twenty-one years. Her books include *The ms of my kin* (Shearsman) and *F2F* (UNDP).

Illinois

Sarah Rosenthal is the author of *The Grass Is Greener When the Sun Is Yellow* (The Operating System, 2019, a collaboration with Valerie Witte), *Lizard* (Chax, 2016), and *Manhatten* (Spuyten Duyvil, 2009), as well as numerous chapbooks. She edited *A Community Writing Itself: Conversations with Vanguard Writers of the Bay Area* (Dalkey Archive, 2010). Her short film *We Agree on the Sun* premiered at the 2019 &Now Festival of Innovative Writing in Bothell, WA. Sarah is the recipient of grant-supported writing residencies at This Will Take Time, Vermont Studio Center, Soul Mountain, Ragdale, New York Mills, and Hambidge. She lives in San Francisco where she works as a Life and Professional Coach, manages programs for the Center for the Collaborative Classroom, and serves on the California Book Awards poetry jury. More at sarahrosenthal.net.

Karen G. (Farnbacher) Hillman (1919–2018)
Karen was born in Augsburg, Germany. After Kristallnacht, she fled to London and empowered herself by working hard despite the trauma of losing her family in the Holocaust. Initially supporting herself as a maid, she eventually earned an undergraduate degree from the London School of Economics and a Master's in Sociology from Northwestern University. She volunteered for Northwestern's international student program and the League of Women Voters, taught in the Osher Lifelong Learning Program, conducted research on fair housing issues, and served on boards of mental health and social service organizations. She is remembered above all for her determination to help change social consciousness, her curious mind, and, with her husband Jay, nurturing connections with friends and extended family.

Indiana

Marianne Boruch has published nine books of poems, most recently *THE ANTI-GRIEF* (Copper Canyon Press, 2019), three essay collections including *The Little Death of Self* (Michigan, 2017), and a memoir, *The Glimpse Traveler* (Indiana, 2011). Her work appears in *The New York Review of Books*, *Poetry*, *The New Yorker*, *American Poetry Review*. Her honors—the Kingsley-Tufts Award, plus fellowships/ residencies from the Guggenheim Foundation, the NEA, the Rockefeller Foundation's Bellagio Center, two natio-nal parks (Denali and Isle Royale). Boruch taught at Purdue University for 31 years and currently teaches in the low-residency Program for Writers at Warren Wilson College.

Iowa

Akwi Nji is a multidisciplinary artist creating in poetry, spoken word, and visual art. Her work and words have appeared on stage from California's Wine Country Festivals to New York's Fashion Week. She is a former Iowa Arts Council Fellow, founder of The Hook, and producer of multimedia artistic events in the Midwest. Her collaborative partners include Emmy Award–winning composers, nationally renowned dancers and choreograp-hers, and companies and organizations ready to think differently about the power of story told through art.

Working together as the Belle Morte Collective based in Des Moines, Iowa, interdisciplinary artist **Larassa Kabel** and photographer **Ben Easter** have been creating performance based photographs for the *Death in the Family* series since the first one appeared in *Juxtapoz Magazine* in 2015. Based in the tradition of Victorian postmortem photography, the *Death in the Family* series critically examines the artificial division humans make between themselves and Nature. The photographs use a powerful combination of beauty and physical tenderness to democratize grief across species and transform each animal into a unique individual worthy of memorialization.

Kansas

Megan Kaminski is a poet and essayist, and the author of three books of poetry, *Gentlewomen* (2020), *Desiring Map* (2015), and *Deep City* (2012). An Associate Professor in the Department of English at the University of Kansas, she teaches classes in poetry, poetics, and the environmental humanities and is Co-director of the KU Global Grasslands CoLABorative. She is also the founder and curator of the Ad Astra Project.

Kentucky

Kristen Renee Miller is the managing editor for *Sarabande*. A poet and translator, she is the 2020 winner of the Gulf Coast Prize in Translation and the translator of two books of poetry from the French by Ilnu Nation poet Marie-Andrée Gill. Her work can be found in *POETRY*, *The Kenyon Review*, *DIAGRAM*, *jubilat*, and *Best New Poets*, and she is the recipient of fellowships and awards from the Foundation for Contemporary Arts, the John F. Kennedy Center for the Performing Arts, and the American Literary Translators Association. She lives in Louisville, Kentucky.

Louisiana

Megan Burns is the publisher at Trembling Pillow Press (tremblingpillowpress.com). She also hosts the Blood Jet Poetry Reading Series in New Orleans and is the co-founder of the New Orleans Poetry Festival (nolapoetry.com). She has been most recently published in *Jacket Magazine*, *Callaloo*, *New Laurel Review*, *Dream Pop*, and *Diagram*. Her poetry and prose reviews have been published in *Tarpaulin Sky*, *Gently Read Lit*, *Big Bridge*, and *Rain Taxi*. She has three books—*Memorial + Sight Lines* (2008), *Sound and Basin* (2013), and *Commitment* (2015)—published by Lavender Ink. She has three recent chapbooks: *Dollbaby* (Horseless Press, 2013), *i always wanted to start over* (Nous- Zot Press, 2014) and her Twin Peaks chap, *Sleepwalk With Me* (Horse Less Press, 2016). Her fourth collection, *BASIC PROGRAMMING*, was published by Lavender Ink in 2018.

Maine

Stuart Kestenbaum is the author of four collections of poems, most recently *Only Now* (Deerbrook Editions), and a collection of essays, *The View From Here* (Brynmorgen Press). The director of the Haystack Mountain School of Crafts from 1988 until 2015, he has written and spoken widely on craft making and creativity, and he's the host of the podcast series *Make/Time*. His poems and writing have appeared in numerous small press publications and magazines including *Tikkun*, the *Sun*, and the *Beloit Poetry Journal*. He was appointed Maine's poet laureate in 2016.

Maryland

Linda Pastan graduated from Radcliffe College, received an MA from Brandeis University and an honorary doctorate from Kenyon College. She has published 14 volumes of poetry, most recently *Insomnia*. Two of these books have been finalists for the National Book Award. She has won numerous awards, including the Radcliffe Distinguished Alumni Award and the Maurice English Award. In 2003 she won the Ruth Lilly Poetry Prize for lifetime achievement. Pastan is a former Poet Laureate of Maryland. Her new book of dog-related poems, *A Dog Runs Through It*, will be published in 2018.

Massachusetts

Eileen Myles came to New York from Boston in 1974 to be a poet, subsequently a novelist, public talker and art journalist. Their twenty-two books include *For Now*, an essay/talk about writing from Yale Press (2020), *evolution* (poems), *Afterglow (a dog memoir)*, a 2017 re-issue of *Cool for You, I Must Be Living Twice/new and selected poems*, and *Chelsea Girls*. They showed their photographs in 2019 at Bridget Donahue, NYC. Eileen is the recipient of a Guggenheim Fellowship, an American Academy of Arts and Letters Award in Literature, an Andy Warhol/Creative Capital Arts Writers grant, four Lambda Book Awards, the Shelley Prize from the PSA, and a poetry award from the Foundation for Contemporary Arts. In 2016, Myles received a Creative Capital grant and the Clark Prize for excellence in art writing. In 2019 they received an award from the American Academy of Arts and Letters. They live in New York and Marfa, TX. Bio photo by Shae Detar.

Michigan

Rob Halpern lives between San Francisco and Ypsilanti, Michigan, where he teaches at Eastern Michigan University and Women's Huron Valley Prison.

Karmyn Valentine resides in Michigan, enjoys private living, and exploring her creativity as an artist and a writer. She has work in the current issue of *BathHouse Journal* and forthcoming in *Detroit Research*. "The great art of life is sensation, to feel that we exist, even in pain" (Lord Byron).

Minnesota

신 선 영 **Sun Yung Shin** was born in Seoul, Korea. She is the author of poetry/essay collections *Unbearable Splendor* (Minnesota Book Award); *Rough, and Savage*; and *Skirt Full of Black* (Asian American Literary Award). She is also the editor of *A Good Time for the Truth: Race in Minnesota*, coeditor of *Outsiders Within: Writing on Transracial Adoption*, and author of bilingual Korean/English illustrated book for children *Cooper's Lesson*. With poet Su Hwang, she cofounded and codirects Poetry Asylum. She lives in Minneapolis with her family.

Mississippi

E. Ethelbert Miller is a literary activist and the author of two memoirs and several books of poetry. Miller was awarded the 2016 AWP George Garrett Award for Outstanding Community Service in Literature and the 2016 DC Mayor's Arts Award for *Distinguished Honor* and appointed in 2018 as an ambassador for the

Authors Guild. *The Collected Poems of E. Ethelbert Miller* (Willow Books, 2016) is a comprehensive collection that represents over 40 years of his career as a poet. Miller's latest book, *If God Invented Baseball* (City Point Press), was awarded the 2019 Literary Award for poetry by the American Library Association's Black Caucus.

Missouri

Dorothea Lasky is the author of several books of poems, including, most recently *Animal* (Wave Books). She teaches poetry at Columbia University's School of the Arts and lives in New York City.

Montana

Prageeta Sharma is the author of the poetry collections *Grief Sequence* (Wave Books, 2019), *Undergloom* (Fence Books, 2013), *Infamous Landscapes* (Fence Books, 2007), *The Opening Question* (Fence Books, 2004), which won the 2004 Fence Modern Poets Prize, and *Bliss to Fill* (Subpress, 2000). She is the founder of the conference Thinking Its Presence: Race, Creative Writing, Literary Studies and Art. A recipient of the 2010 Howard Foundation Award and a finalist for the 2020 Four Quartets Prize, she has taught at the University of Montana and is now the Henry G. Lee '37 Professor of English at Pomona College.

Nebraska

Matt Mason is the Nebraska State Poet and Executive Director of the Nebraska Writers Collective. He has run poetry programs for the state departments in Nepal, Romania, Botswana, and Belarus. Mason is the recipient of a Pushcart Prize and his work can be found in magazines and anthologies including Ted Kooser's *American Life in Poetry*. The author of *Things We Don't Know We Don't Know* (The Backwaters Press, 2006) and *The Baby That Ate Cincinnati* (Stephen F. Austin University Press, 2013), Matt is based out of Omaha with his wife, the poet Sarah McKinstry-Brown, and daughters, Sophia and Lucia.

Tim Guthrie is an Omaha-based multi-media visual artist and experimental filmmaker. He has received multiple Independent Artist Fellowships, including a Distinguished Artist Award from the NEA. He has also presented all over the country and internationally, including the Sorbonne in Paris, France. He was also a TEDx Omaha speaker in 2018.

His film "Missing Piece," garnered dozens of Best Documentary awards, including the 2017 Humanitarian Award (GIFA), Audience Choice and Special Juror's awards and shown widely, including in Wales, UK, Sweden (High Coast), Japan (Hiroshima Animation Festival), Greece (Athens International Animation Festival), Italy (Control Arms Conference), as well in London, Bucharest, Copenhagen, and Toronto.

Nevada

Vogue Robinson—a poet, mentor, teaching artist, and program director—has an appreciation for human beings who find ways to put truth and heart into words. She was named Clark County Nevada's second poet laureate in 2017. Robinson's writing is known to be largely narrative and conversational. Her work has been anthologized in *Sandstone and Silver*, *A Change is Gonna Come*, *Legs of Tumbleweeds*, *Wings of Lace*, and *Clark*. Vogue holds a bachelor's degree in English from San Diego State University. To support this artist, visit her website vogue316.com.

New Hampshire

Kate Greenstreet was born in Chicago. Since then, she has lived in a lot of places on the east and west coasts. She's been in New Hampshire for seven years. Her books are *case sensitive*, *The Last 4 Things*, *Young Tambling*, and *The End of Something*.

New Jersey

Cortney Lamar Charleston is a Cave Canem fellow, a New Jersey State Council of the Arts fellow, and the Pushcart Prize–winning author of *Telepathologies* (Saturnalia Books, 2017) and the forthcoming *Doppelgangbanger* (Haymarket Books, 2021). He currently serves as poetry editor at *The Rumpus* and is a member of the Alice James Books editorial board.

New Mexico

Arthur Sze served as the inaugural poet laureate of Santa Fe, New Mexico, from 2006–2008. He received the 2019 National Book Award for Poetry for *Sight Lines* (Copper Canyon), and his latest book of poetry is *The Glass Constellation: New and Collected Poems* (Copper Canyon, 2021).

New York

Jennifer Firestone is the author of five books of poetry and four chapbooks, including *Story* (UDP), *Ten* (BlazeVOX [books]), *Gates & Fields* (Belladonna* Collaborative), *Swimming Pool* (DoubleCross Press), *Flashes* (Shearsman Books), *Holiday* (Shearsman Books), *Waves* (Portable Press at Yo-Yo Labs), *from Flashes* and *snapshot* (Sona Books) and *Fanimaly* (Dusie Kollektiv). She co-edited (with Dana Teen Lomax) *Letters to Poets: Conversations About Poetics, Politics and Community* (Saturnalia Books) and is collaborating with Marcella Durand on a book about Feminist Avant-garde Poetics. Firestone has work anthologized in *Kindergarde: Avant-garde Poems, Plays, Songs, and Stories for Children* and *Building is a Process / Light is an Element: essays and excursions for Myung Mi Kim*. She won the 2014 Marsh Hawk Press Robert Creeley Memorial Prize. Firestone is an Associate Professor of Literary Studies at the New School's Eugene Lang College and is also the Director of their Academic Fellows pedagogy program.

Ava Firestone-Morrill is a Brooklyn poet, who also dances, sings, and is involved in theater projects.

North Carolina

Pulitzer Prize finalist **Dorianne Laux**'s most recent book is *Only as the Day Is Long: New and Selected Poems*. *The Book of Men* is winner of the Paterson Poetry Prize and *Facts About the Moon* won the Oregon Book Award. Laux is also author of *Awake*, *What We Carry*, and *Smoke* from BOA Editions. She teaches poetry in the MFA Program at North Carolina State University and is founding faculty at Pacific University's Low Residency MFA Program. Bio photo by B.A. Van Sise.

North Dakota

Denise K. Lajimodiere is an enrolled citizen of the Turtle Mountain Band of Ojibwe, Belcourt, ND. A recently retired educator, she worked 44 years as a teacher, principal, and Associate Professional of Educational Leadership at North Dakota State University. Her poetry publications include *Dragonfly Dance*, *Bitter Tears*, and *Thunderbird*. Her academic book about the tragedy of the era of American Indian boarding schools titled *Stringing Rosaries* was published in 2019. Her latest full-length book of poetry, *His Feathers Were Chains*, appeared in 2020, and a children's book, *Josie Dances*, was published in 2021. Lajimodiere's work has won numerous awards.

Northern Mariana Islands

Joey "Pepe Batbon" Connolly is a retired public school English teacher on Tinian, Commonwealth of Northern Mariana Islands (CNMI), at 15 degrees north latitude. He enjoys stargazing, writing poetry, and watching *chunge'* birds circle in pairs overhead. *Chunge'* is the Chamorro language word for a white-tailed tropic bird— *Phaeton lepturus dorotheae*. Joey "Pepe Batbon" Connolly is the Poet Laureate of Tinian, CNMI.

Ohio

Amit Majmudar's newest poetry collection is *What He Did in Solitary* (Knopf, 2020). He served as Ohio's first Poet Laureate and works as a diagnostic nuclear radiologist in Westerville, Ohio, where he lives with his wife, twin sons, and daughter.

Savya Majmudar is a thirteen-year-old math whiz who loves Chipotle and chess. This is his first published photograph.

Oklahoma

Joy Harjo is the author of nine books of poetry, including her recent *An American Sunrise*. She has been honored with the Ruth Lilly Prize from the Poetry Foundation, the Wallace Stevens Award from the Academy of American Poets, and a Guggenheim Fellowship. Her memoir *Crazy Brave* won the PEN USA Literary Award. In 2019 she was appointed the 23rd U.S. Poet Laureate and was reappointed to a second term. She lives in Tulsa, Oklahoma, where she is a Tulsa Artist Fellow. Bio photo by Karen Kuehn.

Oregon

Douglas Manuel was born in Anderson, Indiana. He received a BA in Creative Writing from Arizona State University and an MFA from Butler University where he was the Managing Editor of the journal *Booth*. He is currently a Middleton and Dornsife Fellow at the University of Southern California where he is pursuing a PhD in Literature and Creative Writing. He has served as the Poetry Editor for Gold Line Press as well as one of the Managing Editors of Ricochet Editions. His poems are featured on the Poetry Foundation's website and have appeared or are forthcoming in *Pleiades*, *Poetry Northwest*, *The Los Angeles Review*, *Superstition Review*, *Rhino*, *North American Review*, *The Chattahoochee Review*, *New Orleans Review*, *Crab Creek Review*, and elsewhere. His first full-length collection of poems, *Testify* (Red Hen Press, 2017), won an IBPA Benjamin Franklin Award for poetry. In 2020, he received the Dana Gioia Poetry Award.

Pennsylvania

The author of six full-length poetry books, **Raquel Salas Rivera**'s honors include being named the 2018–19 Poet Laureate of Philadelphia and receiving the New Voices Award, the Lambda Literary Award, the Ambroggio Prize, and an NEA Translation Fellowship. He has also been long-listed for the 2018 National Book Award and the 2020 PEN America Open Book Award. He holds a Ph.D. in Comparative Literature and Literary Theory from the University of Pennsylvania and currently works as an investigator for El proyecto de la literatura puertorriqueña/The Puerto Rican Literature Project.

Raquel Salas Rivera es el autor de seis poemarios. Sus reconocimientos incluyen el nombramiento como Poeta Laureado de la ciudad de Filadelfia, el Premio Nuevas Voces, el Premio Literario Lambda, el inaugural Premio Ambroggio, la beca de Poeta Laureado y una beca de Traducción del NEA. Ha sido semifinalista para el National Book Award del 2018 y el PEN America Open Book Award del 2020. Obtuvo un Doctorado en Literatura Comparada y Teoría Literaria de la Universidad de Pensilvania y sirve de investigador y supervisor del equipo de traducción para *El proyecto de la literatura puertorriqueña/ The Puerto Rican Literature Project*.

Puerto Rico

Julio César Pol was born in August 1976 in Ponce, Puerto Rico. He was Director of the magazine *El Sótano 00931* and General Coordinator of the meetings of (De) Generaciones. He is the editor of the anthology *Los rostros de la Hidra* (2008) with the houses of Isla Negra Editores and Ediciones Gaviota y Poesía de Puerto Rico: Cinco Décadas. His books *La luz necesaria* (2006), *Idus de Marzo* (2008), *Mardi Gras* (2012), and *Sísifo* (2017) were published under the seal of Isla Negra Editores. He holds a PhD in Economics. See more at juliocesarpol.com.

Rhode Island

Sawako Nakayasu is an artist working with language, performance, and translation—separately and in various combinations. She has lived mostly in the U.S. and Japan, briefly in France and China, and she translates from Japanese. Her books include *Some Girls Walk into the Country They Are From* (Wave Books), *Pink Waves* (forthcoming, Omnidawn), and *The Ants* (Les Figues Press). She is co-editor, with Lisa Samuels, of *A Transpacific Poetics*, a gathering of poetry and poetics engaging transpacific imaginaries. She teaches at Brown University.

South Carolina

Marcus Amaker was named the first Poet Laureate of Charleston, SC, in 2016. In 2021, he became an Academy of American Poets fellow. He's also an award-winning graphic designer, an electronic musician, and a mentor. His poetry has been recognized by the Kennedy Center, *American Poets Magazine*, the Washington National Opera, *Button Poetry*, NPR, *The Chicago Tribune*, Edutopia, and more. In 2019, he won a Governor's Arts award in South Carolina, and was named the artist-in-residence of the Gaillard Center. Marcus has recorded three albums with Grammy Award-winning artist Quentin E. Baxter. His ninth book is *Black Music Is*.

South Dakota

Lee Ann Roripaugh's most recent book is *tsunami vs. the fukushima 50* (Milkweed Editions, 2019). The South Dakota State Poet Laureate from 2015–2019, Roripaugh is a Professor of English at the University of South Dakota, where she serves as Director of Creative Writing and Editor-in-Chief of *South Dakota Review*.

Tennessee

Ama Codjoe is the author of *Blood of the Air* (Northwestern University Press, 2020), winner of the Drinking Gourd Chapbook Poetry Prize, and *Bluest Nude*, forthcoming from Milkweed Editions in 2022. She has been awarded support from the Cave Canem, Robert Rauschenberg, and Saltonstall foundations as well as from the Callaloo Creative Writing Workshop, Hedgebrook, Yaddo, and MacDowell. Her recent poems have appeared in *The Best American Poetry* and elsewhere. Among other honors, Codjoe has received fellowships from the National Endowment for the Arts, the New York State Council/New York Foundation of the Arts, and the Jerome Foundation.

Texas

Ching-In Chen is the author of *The Heart's Traffic*, *recombinant* (winner of the 2018 Lambda Literary Award for Transgender Poetry), *how to make black paper sing* and *Kundiman for Kin :: Information Retrieval for Monsters*. Chen is also the co-editor of *The Revolution Starts at Home: Confronting Intimate Violence Within Activist Communities*. They have received fellowships from Kundiman, Lambda, Watering Hole, Can Serrat and Imagining America and are a part of Macondo and Voices of Our Nations Arts Foundation writing communities. While faculty at Sam Houston State University, they served as poetry editor of the *Texas Review*. They currently teach creative writing at the University of Washington Bothell.

Cassie Mira is a transgender artist, technologist, and curator whose practice explores liminal space, human interaction, and transitional experience.

U.S. Virgin Islands

Tiphanie Yanique is the author of the poetry collection *Wife*, which won the 2016 Bocas Prize in Caribbean Poetry and the United Kingdom's 2016 Forward/Felix Dennis Prize for a First Collection. Tiphanie is also the author of the novel *Land of Love and Drowning*, which won the 2014 Flaherty-Dunnan First Novel Award, the Phillis Wheatley Award for Pan-African Literature, and the American Academy of Arts and Letters Rosenthal Family Foundation Award. She is also the author of a collection of stories, *How to Escape from a Leper Colony*, which won her a listing as one of the National Book Foundation's 5Under35. Her writing has also won the Bocas Award for Caribbean Fiction, the Boston Review Prize in Fiction, a Rona Jaffe Foundation Writers Award, a Pushcart Prize, a Fulbright Scholarship, and an Academy of American Poet's Prize. She has been listed by the *Boston Globe* as one of the sixteen cultural figures to watch out for and her writing has been published in the *New York Times*, *Best African American Fiction*, *the Wall Street Journal*, *American Short Fiction*, and other places. Tiphanie is from the Virgin Islands and currently teaches English and Creative Writing at Emory College of Arts and Sciences. For more about Tiphanie, check out "Race, Power and Storytelling: An Interview with Tiphanie Yanique" in *Kweli*.

Utah

Craig Dworkin is the author, most recently, of *The Pine-Woods Notebook* (Kenning, 2019). He teaches literary history at the University of Utah and serves as Founding Senior Editor to the Eclipse archive at eclipsearchive.org.

Vermont

Camille Guthrie's new book, *Diamonds*, is forthcoming from BOA Editions in 2021. She is the author of *Articulated Lair: Poems for Louise Bourgeois* (Subpress 2013). Her new poems have appeared in *At Length*, the *Boston Review*, *The Iowa Review*, *Interim*, *The New Republic*, and *Tin House*. She is the Director of Undergraduate Writing at Bennington College. She lives in Bennington, VT, with her two kids.

Virginia

Richmond, VA, native **giovanni singleton** is the author of the poetry book *Ascension* and the poetry/art collection *AMERICAN LETTERS: works on paper*. She won the California Book Award Gold and received the African American Literature and Culture Society's Stephen E. Henderson Award. She is founding editor of *nocturnes (re)view of the literary arts*, a journal of the African Diaspora and other contested spaces.

Washington

Samuel and Sally Green reside on Waldron Island, where they have been the co-publishers of Brooding Heron Press & Bindery for the past 38 years, producing fine, letter-pressed volumes of poetry written or translated by contemporary poets. Sally's most recent collection of poems is *Full Immersion* (Expedition Press, 2014); Sam's is *Disturbing the Light* (Carnegie Mellon University Press, 2020). Sam served two years as Washington's inaugural poet laureate.

Cora Green, Sam and Sally's granddaughter, also lives on Waldron. Having graduated from the eighth grade—the limit of the tiny island school—she is now homeschooling for her first year of high school. She is an avid photographer, a musician, and a budding graphic artist. She has already won prizes for her poems.

Washington, D.C.

San Francisco poet **Sarah Anne Cox** was born in the Columbia Hospital for Women in D.C., and is the author of *Arrival*, Krupsaya 2002, *Parcel*, O Books 2006, and *Super Undone Blue*, Dusie 2016. Her work has appeared in the American anthologies *Bay Poetics*, *Technologies of Measure*, and *Kindergarde*, which won the Johns Hopkins University Press Lion & Unicorn Award. In 2014, her poems were translated into Swedish by Kristian Carlsson. She studies classics at Edinburgh, teaches writing at SFSU, and windsurfs and snowboards with her unschooled family.

West Virginia

Marc Harshman's collection of poems *WOMAN IN A RED ANORAK* won the Blue Lynx Prize published by Lynx House/University of Washington Press in 2018. His 14th children's book, *FALLINGWATER*, co-written with Anna Smucker, and an Amazon Book of the Month, was published by Roaring Brook/Macmillan in 2017. His poetry collection *BELIEVE WHAT YOU CAN*, published in 2016 by West Virginia University Press, won the Weatherford Award from the Appalachian Studies Association. Poems have been anthologized by Kent State University, the University of Iowa, University of Georgia, and the University of Arizona. He has most recently been named co-winner of the 2019 Allen Ginsberg Poetry Award and continues as 7th poet laureate of West Virginia.

Wisconsin

Oliver Baez Bendorf is the author of *Advantages of Being Evergreen* (winner of the CSU Poetry Center Open Book Poetry Competition), which Gabrielle Calvocoressi called "an essential book for our time and for all time," and *The Spectral Wilderness*, selected by Mark Doty for the Stan & Tom Wick Poetry Prize. Oliver received the 2020 Betty Berzon Emerging Writer Award from The Publishing Triangle. Born and raised in Iowa, he was the 2017–2018 Halls Emerging Artist Fellow at University of Wisconsin-Madison's Institute for Creative Writing, where he taught queer poetics and co-founded the studio space EVERYDAY GAY HOLIDAY. He also holds an MFA in Poetry and an MA in Library and Information Studies from UW-Madison. A CantoMundo fellow, Oliver is currently an assistant professor of poetry at Kalamazoo College in Michigan. Bio photo by Faylita Hicks.

Wyoming

David Romtvedt's poetry collection *No Way: An American Tao Te Ching* is forthcoming from LSU in spring 2021. His translations of the nineteenth-century Basque poet Joxe Mari Iparragirre appeared in 2020 from the Center for Basque Studies at the University of Nevada. Past books include the poetry collection *Dilemmas of the Angels* (LSU, 2017) and the novel *Zelestina Urza in Outer Space* (U of Nevada CBS, 2015). His collection *A Flower Whose Name I Do Not Know* was selected for the National Poetry Series. A recipient of two NEA fellowships, two Wyoming Arts Council fellowships, the Pushcart Prize, and the Wyoming Governor's Arts Award, he served for seven years as poet laureate of Wyoming. With the Fireants, Romtvedt has released three recordings—*Bury My Clothes*, *Ants on Ice*, and *It's Hot*. With Ospa, he's recorded *Hori da*, traditional Basque music.

Born and raised in the Basque community of Wyoming, **Caitlin Belem Romtvedt** has also lived in Brazil where she studied capoeira and music. She performs Basque music with the band Ospa and Brazilian and Latin American music with Maracujá. She is currently a PhD candidate in ethnomusicology at the University of California at Berkeley.

The Introduction

"All Is Beautiful"

Son of farmworkers, **Juan Felipe** lives in Fresno with his wife, poet Margarita Robles. During the last fifty years, he has dedicated his life to poetry, community, art and teaching. In the last ten years, he has been the Poet Laureate of California and of the United States. Various awards include the National Book Critic's Circle Award, Guggenheim Fellowship, LA Times Robert Kirsch Award, Latino Hall of Fame Award, Pushcart Prize and UCLA Chancellor's Medal. With over thirty books in various genres, his recent work is *Every Day We Get More Illegal* (City Lights Publishers). He is a graduate of UCLA, Stanford, and the University of Iowa Writer's Workshop. Bio photo by Carlos Puma, UC Riverside.

About the Visual Artists

Yreina D. Cervántez is a Professor Emeritus in the Department of Chicana/o Studies at California State University at Northridge, teaching from 1999–2019. Through her art, teaching and community activism, she has contributed to the discourse on an ever-evolving Chicanx aesthetic. Her work speaks to issues of decolonization, the intersection of spirituality, politics, and Xicana-Indigena feminist identity and empowerment. Her art is in various collections including the Smithsonian American Art Museum, the L.A. County Museum of Art, the National Museum of Mexican Art in Chicago, Illinois, the Blanton Museum of Art, UT Austin, and others. Bio photo by Marialice Jacob.

Norma Cole's most recent books of poetry are *Win These Posters and Other Unrelated Prizes Inside* (Omnidawn), *Where Shadows Will: Selected Poems 1988–2008* (City Lights) and *NATURAL LIGHT* (Libellum). Her book of essays and talks, *TO BE AT MUSIC,* has appeared from Omnidawn Press. Cole has received awards from the Gerbode Foundation, Gertrude Stein Awards, the Fund for Poetry and the Foundation for Contemporary Arts. She teaches at the University of San Francisco.

Stephen Lovekin has been a Staff Photographer with Shutterstock since 2015. He has over 20 years of professional experience and has photographed such high-profile events as the Academy Awards, the Golden Globes, the Tony's, New York Fashion Week, the Toronto Film Festival, and many others. His work has been published in publications like the *New York Times*, *Variety*, *WWD*, *Rolling Stone*, *Vogue*, *Elle*, *Vanity Fair*, *InStyle*, *People*, *Us Weekly*, and more. He also has a particular interest in shooting portraits as well as news. Stephen currently resides in Brookly with his wife, Kristin, and their two children, Lucas and Callie.

THE BEAUTIFUL cover artist, **Amber Robles-Gordon**, is a mixed media visual artist, of Puerto Rican and West Indian heritage. Robles-Gordon, has over twenty years of exhibiting, art education, commissioned critiques, lectures, art commentary and exhibition coordinating experience. She received a Bachelor of Science, Business Administration in 2005 at Trinity University, and subsequently a Master's in Fine Arts (Painting) in 2011 from Howard University, Washington, DC. She has exhibited nationally and in Germany, Italy, Malaysia, London, and Spain. Robles-Gordon has been commissioned to create temporary, permanent public art installations for numerous art fairs, universities, government agencies, art galleries and institutions. Additionally, she has been commissioned and or featured to teach workshops, give commentary, and or present about her artwork for various television and radio stations, museums, universities/colleges, podcasts and art organizations.

Sherry Shine has always had the ability to draw, and while in high school, she had an art teacher that cultivated her and was a strong mentor. Many years after high school, Sherry decided to focus on her skills as an artist, and she went back to school and took some courses in art but was still unsure of what to with her talent. Then one day a friend invited her to try quilting after going to a lecture together on the subject of the "art quilt." Sherry then began learning all about traditional quilting, including cutting and piecing of fabrics along with the history of quilting. This was the foundation for her career as a fiber artist.

Hiroshi Sugimoto was born in 1948 in Japan and divides his time between Tokyo and New York City. Primarily a photographer since the 1970s, Sugimoto more recently added performing arts production and architecture to his multidisciplinary practice, which deals with history and temporal existence by investigating themes of time, empiricism, and metaphysics. Grounded in technical mastery of the classical photographic tradition, his work has explored the ways photography can record traces of invisible but elemental forces. Bio photo © Hiroshi Sugimoto (*Self Portrait*, 2019), courtesy of Fraenkel Gallery, San

About the Project Consultants

Una Lomax-Emrick is a writer based in Rhode Island and California. Their work focuses on family systems and the natural world.

Jill Stengel began a+bend press in 1999, producing chapbooks in conjunction with a monthly reading series in San Francisco. a+bend press was very prolific, producing 40 chapbooks in 20 months, and publishing new and established authors including Jen Hofer, Tisa Bryant, Elizabeth Treadwell, and Kathleen Fraser. Jill herself became even more prolific and had three children. Jill's full-length collection *Dear Jack* was published in 2013, and she has authored 12 chapbooks. (See jillstengel.com for details.) In 2019, a+bend press produced its first book with a spine.

Francisco."

About the Interns

Claire "Champagne" Champommier is a proud lesbian Asian American creative and artist. Currently a student, she has studied writing at Lewis & Clark College. Her work has appeared in *Interim*, *Otis Nebula*, *SPLASH!* (from Haunted Waters Press), the *Tiger Moth Review*, *Fleas on the Dog*, *Feels Blind Literary*, and *Auroras & Blossoms*. She is the San Franciscan winner for *smART Magazine*'s poetry competition. She's sending hugs to her friends and family from her room in Portland, Oregon.

Julia Wong is a Bay Area–raised poet and artist studying in her first year at the University of California, Berkeley. Her poetry has been published in an anthology titled *There Are Greater Songs Than Love Songs* by the Marin Poetry Center.

Charlie Julian is an artist, a writer, and an activist. They are the recipient of the Golden Heart Award given by the Davis City Council and the first-ever Mikey Partida Realizing Resilience Award given by The Phoenix Coalition. Charlie lives in Davis, California, with a cat and several plants.

About the Designer

Roberta Morris ('Berta) is a San Francisco–based designer with many years of experience in publishing. As the Founder and Creative Director of Leave It to 'Berta (leaveittoberta.com), she works closely with publishers and authors on projects ranging from curriculum to memoirs—helping to bring their publications and stories to life. 'Berta is honored to have received numerous design awards, including a 2020 Purple Dragonfly Award in Children's Nonfiction for *Robert Wadlow: The Unique Life of the Boy Who Became the World's Tallest Man* and a 2020 Royal Dragonfly Award in Young Adult Nonfiction for *Elijay Lovejoy's Fight for Freedom*, both historical biographies by author Jennifer Phillips. 'Berta regularly gives back to the community by volunteering for organizations such as Career Girls and Taproot Foundation. She also enjoys writing about all things colorful and creative via her Martini Minute blog (medium.com/martini-minute). When she's not designing something, she pursues other interests such as world travel, painting and collage, crochet, science, reading, writing, gardening, adventurous cuisine, artisanal coffee, karaoke, and cats.

About the Publisher

Gualala Arts is a community arts organization, located in Gualala, California, dedicated to promoting public interest and participation in the arts since 1961. Gualala Arts coordinates art exhibits, workshops and classes, classical and popular music performances, theater, lectures, publishing projects, and much more. Please find them at gualalaarts.org.

Norma Cole. *Untitled*. 2016, oil pastel on paper.
From *Norma Cole, DRAWINGS* (Further Other Book
Works, 2020). © Norma Cole.

ACKNOWLEDGMENTS

This anthology, by design, is a collaborative effort. I am grateful to everyone who agreed to participate, trusted me with their work, and jumped into this interdependent project. I am thankful for what we have made together. These poets demonstrate a generosity that is beautiful in itself. I would also like to send my gratitude to the visual artists whose work appears in this volume. Each of their pieces turns the simplest moment into a work of ecstatic beauty. To everyone who participated in this anthology, I thank you for your vision and for your inspiration.

In the process of writing the Editor's Note, I realized how much I rely on the strength, spirit, and ideas of my mentors, especially Claire Braz-Valentine, Myung Mi Kim, and Norma Cole. Their commitment to the urgency of poetry, to its art and responsibility, and to an extended sense of the communal I've never forgotten.

I would also like to thank the artist Dread Scott, who, although we've never met, helped me distill a running theme on beauty in this work. In the final stages of completing *THE BEAUTIFUL*, I listened to a June 24, 2020, Artnet Talks presentation titled "Art as an Act of Resistance: A Conversation With Shaun Leonardo, Dread Scott, and Clifford Owens." In it, Scott says, "Recently I've been thinking a lot about not depicting trauma but actually depicting liberation and resistance . . . But I also think this question of 'Do we just need to reflect the trauma we are suffering for/from in a daily experience, or do we actually also need to show a way out of this nightmare?' And I do not think it's an 'either/or.' I think it's an 'and.'" After hearing Scott talk about his work, I appreciated his articulation of beauty as "a way out of this nightmare." As a coconspirator and an activist artist, I am very grateful for these words.

In addition, I would like to thank the late artist Félix González-Torres. His 1991 piece *Untitled (Portrait of Ross in L.A.)* serves as a reminder of the bittersweetness in any loss, in any tragedy, at any given time. The lingering love is always there—if only in fragments—and it still can consume us in memory, in moments of pure joy.

Also, I am grateful for Katherine McKittrick's work. In *Dear Science and Other Stories*, she invites readers to reimagine inherited narratives, collaborate across fields, bend the disciplines, open the door to poetry and music (no matter the genre of their particular projects), offer a playlist on their websites, credit everybody and everything they learn from, reminding me that creativity and collectivity are the answer to most any question.

I am indebted to Peter Krohn, a Holocaust survivor and speaker with the Sonoma Story Project. Originally from Germany, Krohn lost most of his family during the Holocaust. In his 70s, he had a desire to "paint" the beauty around him. Krohn scans images of vivid botanicals against a black background, the darkness symbolizing the experiences and history he survived. The rich textures and colors of plant life have helped him "to be open and receptive to an unknown, emerging experience." He writes, "I think of this state of mind as one of 'artful presence and observation.' It offers us an opportunity to shift our consciousness away from yesterday's fears and tomorrow's worries, towards a place where our well-being resides." Krohn uses beauty to experience a deeper awareness of the present moment and also to inspire healing and hope—all through the creation of, the expression of, beauty. Meeting him was a gift that fueled this project.

Without the many physicians who cared for me over the years—Dr. Mary Arnold; Dr. Kerry Cho; Dr. Anna Haemel; Thia Haselton, MFT; Dr. Christine Gazulis; Dr. Sarah Goglin; Howard Lunche, MSW, LCSW; Dr. Adrian Jaffer; Dr. Efrem Korngold; Dr. Yamin Nibbe; Dr. Kenneth Sack; Gordon Smith, LMT; Dr. Jonathan Terdiman; Dr. Chris Young and Joe Young, LMT—this work would not be possible. These doctors have kept me alive in more ways than one. I know how fortunate I have been to be in their care.

Many thanks to Henry Frank whom I consulted regarding citing the Navajo/Diné prayer and whose open spirit and kindness have fed my family throughout this year's pandemic. Henry, our family is so grateful for you and Diana.

Thanks also to Niki Sandoval, who without having met me previously, offered sound suggestions regarding the Editor's Note as well as sage wisdom regarding Native peoples: "We don't need to be saved." Her honesty and generosity came my way at an opportune moment and inspired a sense of dignity and respect, just when I needed it.

Much gratitude to Claire Blotter, Duane BigEagle, and Sasha Keller, who were willing to help me out in the final hours before publication and offered keen advice about paring down the Editor's Note. I leaned on them, and they were there for me. I am so thankful.

I must also acknowledge my writing group—Mary Burger, Carrie Hunter, Denise Newman, and Sarah Rosenthal—who have offered incredible insights about almost every aspect of this anthology. I am honored to know and work with these compelling artists. Their commitment to art and activism and their raw honesty about how to grow through artistic practice continues to serve as a source of creative possibilities.

ACKNOWLEDGMENTS *(continued)*

Many thanks to the artists who endorsed this work—F. Douglas Brown, Shane McCrae, Jill Darling, Traci Gourdine, Jennifer Karmin, Eléna Rivera, Srikanth Reddy, and Magdalena Zurawski. Your work prompted me to reach out, and your kindness enriches this anthology.

There are also a number of friends whose advice I sought in the making of *THE BEAUTIFUL*, those who listened to my concerns about the project and helped me keep the faith as time kept ticking on. These include Nicole Brodsky, Laurie Brooks, Janet Cerni, Catherine Chase, Christine Childress, Sarah Anne Cox, Melissa Eleftherion Carr, Jennifer Firestone, Tim Fitzmaurice, Susana Gardner, Richard Ingram (who suggests, "radically informed civil coalescence might be the better path" and "Resist bourgeois scum in their murderous search for authenticity"), Andrea Jagger-Wells, Connie King, Joan Larkin, Mark Latiner, Sarah Weller Leipsic, Lisa Linnenkohl, Brian Lynch, Nicole Mauro, Stephen Motika, Akwi Nji, Sapuro Rayphand, Marthe Reed (in memoriam), Vicki Reno, giovanni singleton, RuthAnn Spike, Jane Sprague, Jill Stengel, Sweet, and Eileen Tabios. Thanks, everyone! It's incredible to have people who love and support us like family. I look forward to hugging you once it's safe.

Many thanks to everyone at the Banff Centre for the Arts and Cel del Nord artist residencies, particularly Jordan Able, Derek Beaulieu, Odette Brady, Nadine Heller, Kaie Kellough, Sarah Rosenthal, Dani Spinosa, Shireen Talhounie, Lea Thijs, and Ilyn Wong. Art in community is the best kind of party!

I also want to thank Claire "Champagne" Champommier, Julia Wong, and Charlie Julian, who were interns for the project and are poets in their own right. These amazing artists brought insights, revision suggestions, careful readings, line edits, and a lot of energy to the project just when I needed it.

Much gratitude also goes out to Lauren Schiffman, who in the final moments was willing to help me fine-tune the Editor's Note for *THE BEAUTIFUL*. Her incredible skill and incomparable knowledge of both the poetic style and written conventions of the English language helped me complete it once and for all. (Any errors found there are thanks to my inability to stop tweaking things and do not reflect her efforts.)

My tremendous thanks goes to Roberta Morris, who designed this book and embraced the project as a true collaborator. Roberta's vision, patience, and willingness to get down and dirty in the process of making this anthology have been invaluable. Roberta is the reason this anthology is a work of beauty in itself. Many thanks to Leave It to 'Berta for this anthology's design in its final form.

I am deeply grateful to the staff and board at Gualala Arts for publishing and supporting this project. David "Sus" Susalla said "yes" to *THE BEAUTIFUL* from the minute I approached him and has supported every aspect of the project. I have always held high hopes for the reach of the anthology, and Sus offered even more expansive ideas and made resources available to help the anthology realize them. Sus once told me that his self-described passion is helping artists bring their visions to life, and he has certainly been instrumental in ushering THE BEAUTIFUL into the world. Many thanks are also due to Kendra Stillman who works tirelessly behind the scenes and ensures that the paperwork is complete, the business cards are printed, the documents are signed, and order dwells in the chaos. Thanks Kendra for making even the logistics fun and creative processes. Special thanks to Bob Mitchell who helped me put together the project's website where the exhibition details and related curriculum will live. Thanks, Bob!

During the pandemic and amidst the distressing news that seemed to keep pouring into our home, our family pets—Quinn, Jacko Reily, and Wilder (after Gene)—brought us continual joy and comfort. In the making of this anthology, they provided constant companionship and important perspective refocusing. I am deeply indebted to them and to the veterinarians who care for them, Dr. Pfiel at the Gualala Vet Clinic, everyone at the Larkspur Vet Hospital, the badass renegade women at FIP Warriors, and the incredibly cool and amazingly singular "Cat Doctor," Kendra Decile. These Docs of Veterinary Medicine have enriched our lives by helping our beloved pets live healthy, happy lives.

Finally, I want to thank my family both living and dead for showing me the importance of community. These loving people have helped me develop a communal poetics and taught me the gift of working closely with others to envision and create the world we want. From them, I've learned that audacity, integrity, humility, passion, imagination, anger, honestly, and forgiveness are all part of beauty.

Many thanks to my in-laws, Alice, Joe, and Tio Steve, who are amazing supporters and loving family, especially since they "got one for the price of two."

All my love and gratitude to Cisco, June, and Marissa, whose beauty is a source of joy always.

Special thanks to Danna, who is my better half. To come into the world with another—I can think of nothing more beautiful, and then, wow, it's Danna!

Thank you, Steven, for your love over the years and your belief in my ideas; even though life takes strange turns, beauty remains.

And Una, I realize how much my projects have become your projects. Your counsel on every aspect of this work has helped me shape and realize it. You have taught me that admiration is an appreciation of beauty but that respect is a deeper understanding of it. Thank you for enriching my life; everything is so much more beautiful with you.

Sugimoto, Hiroshi. *Franklin Park Theater, Boston*, 2015. Photograph.
© Hiroshi Sugimoto, courtesy Fraenkel Gallery, San Francisco.

ABOUT THE EDITOR

Photo by Sarah Weller Leipsic

Dana Teen Lomax is a multi-genre artist and activist. The author of several poetry books and numerous chapbooks, her last editorial project, *Kindergarde: Avant-garde Poems, Plays, Stories, and Songs for Children* (Black Radish Books), was awarded a San Francisco Creative Work Fund Grant and won the 2014 Johns Hopkins University Press Lion and Unicorn Prize for Excellence in North American Poetry. With Jennifer Firestone, she edited *Letters to Poets: Conversations About Poetics, Politics, and Community* (Saturnalia), which Cornel West called a "courageous and visionary book." Dana's writing has been nominated for a Pushcart Prize, published and anthologized internationally, named among the Guerilla Girls' favorite poetry books, and received grants and awards from Intersection for the Arts, the Academy of American Poets, the California Arts Council, the San Francisco Foundation, the Marin Arts Council, the Banff Centre for Arts and Creativity, Cel del Nord, and other organizations. Lomax collaborates with artists from all over the country; has taught writing in libraries, schools, prisons, and universities; and served as the Human Rights and Equity Chair for her teachers' union. She lives in Northern California with her family. Dana's writing, editorial work, and short films can be found at danateenlomax.com.